Dealing with Depression

DEALING WITH DEPRESSION

*Whatever you're going through,
we'll go through it with you*

Trevor Barnes
with The Samaritans

VERMILION
LONDON

A percentage of all royalties received goes to
The Samaritans

1 3 5 7 9 10 8 6 4 2

Copyright © Trevor Barnes 1996

Trevor Barnes has asserted his moral right to be identified as the
author of this work in accordance with the Copyright, Design and
Patents Act 1988.

First published in the United Kingdom in 1996 by Vermilion
an imprint of Ebury Press
Random House UK Ltd
Random House
20 Vauxhall Bridge Road
London SW1V 2SA

Random House Australia (Pty) Ltd
20 Alfred Street, Milsons Point, Sydney,
New South Wales 2061, Australia

Random House New Zealand Limited
18 Poland Rd, Glenfield,
Auckland 10, New Zealand

Random House, South Africa (Pty) Limited
Box 2263, Rosebank 2121, South Africa

Random House UK Limited Reg. No. 954009

A CIP catalogue record for this book is available from the
British Library.

ISBN 0 09 181363 8

Typeset in Palatino

Printed and bound in Great Britain by Mackays of Chatham plc

Papers used by Vermilion are natural, recyclable products made
from wood grown in sustainable forests.

Contents

For S. B.

Trevor Barnes is a writer and broadcaster. He is author of *Man With A Mission*, a biography of Terry Waite and presenter of Radio 4 religious current affairs programme 'Sunday'.

This book was researched by Trevor Barnes as an independent journalist with the cooperation of The Samaritans.

The Samaritans is a registered charity, founded in 1953. The Samaritans is available, 24 hours a day, to provide confidential and emotional support to anyone passing through crisis and at risk of suicide. The Samaritans aims to provide society with a better understanding of suicide and the value of expressing feelings that may lead to suicide.

In 1995 there were over 200 branches in the United Kingdom and Eire, 22,000 volunteers and 3.75 million contacts.

To speak to a Samaritan call 0345 90 90 90 (calls charged at local rate) or Local Branches can be found in the phone book under 'S'.

General Office
10 The Grove
Slough SL1 1QP

Tel: 01753 532713
Fax: 01753 819004

Patron   HRH The Duchess of Kent
Chief Executive   Simon Armson
Chairperson   Jenny Cunnington

Foreword

Depression, to a greater or lesser extent, affects every one of us during the course of our lives; from the depression that simply makes the world appear a grey, uncomfortable place to the deep depression that makes the option of taking our own lives seem the only possible solution.

Receiving three and a half million calls a year, The Samaritans are only too aware that depression destroys the quality of life. It is disabling and can be life threatening. Trevor Barnes explores the whole problem of depression with clarity and insight. Here is a book which will enable those who suffer and those who care for the sufferers to acknowledge the problem, to examine it, and, hopefully to embark on the journey towards recovery.

Jenny Cunnington
Chairman, The Samaritans

Introduction

Congratulations! You have dared to pick up and open a book on depression. Perhaps you are depressed. Perhaps you are not, but are worried about someone close to you who is. Either way you have recognised and acknowledged that all is not right with the world and taken a step to confront the problem. And that is why you are to be congratulated. Recognition and acknowledgement are the first and most daunting steps to take on the road to mental health. And having taken them, you have cleared the first hurdle at which so many fall.

If you have never been seriously depressed yourself, these accounts of the experience may seem strange and exaggerated. If you have known depression then what follows will be horribly familiar.

❝For a seven-month stretch I felt suicidal for most of every day. Often without any cause I would feel full of despair and anguish. In my mind's eye I saw a blanket black colour – like a backcloth to my thoughts. I was frequently debilitated by a profound lethargy and a resistance to physical movement. This felt like having dark lead weights clamping down my legs and torso. Moreover I was frightened of physical activity, as this stimulated my thought processes which could then dwell more intensely on pain and despair. So I deliberately tried to muffle my mental activity by lying in bed. I tried to sleep between 7pm and midday five days a week. And, if on my own, at the weekend I would stay in bed all day and night. It was a constant struggle to get out of bed at all and go to work. Sometimes, when alone, I would collapse to the floor, weeping uncontrollably or imploring anything that would listen to ease my anguish. Of course this brought no relief. My pain was amplified by an excruciating awareness of the slow passage of minutes, or even seconds. Not only did this make me aware of the crushing magnitude of my depression over each moment but I found it almost impossible to believe that I could endure the utter torment of that specific moment and of the future beyond it. **'**

Ellen, 25, Oxford postgraduate now on sickness benefit

Each experience of depression is unique. The sufferer feels alone in a personal nightmare beyond the reach of family or friends. This terrifying isolation, perhaps the most corrosive feature of depressive illness, is what makes the experience so painful to bear – and the condition so difficult to treat.

Treatment and self-help are possible but this book does not underestimate the heroic efforts some people will have to make to believe it. On the days when the depression has lifted a little they may know full well what they *ought* to do; when depression has settled on them they are simply incapable of doing it. Here, the classic symptoms are painfully recalled:

' It was a horrible feeling. A feeling of unhappiness and fear at the same time. I was tired all the time. I went to bed early to escape the day but couldn't sleep. My eyes were shut but my mind was awake. My face was tense and drawn in the morning. I didn't want to get up and face another day. I couldn't concentrate on anything. I got a craze for sweet things because I didn't want to cook. I had no interest in anything. I was always crying. **'**

Rita, 51, housewife

In picking up this book you may have embarked on a long and difficult road. For some it may never end. But you need not be alone as you make the journey into the light. You will travel at your own pace and arrive in your own time but, to say it again, you need not be alone.

That, in short, is the aim of this book. To state that there is always someone there to listen; always someone there to share what it is that you are going through while you are going through it. Along the way you may learn something about the varieties of depression and the multiplicity of its causes. You may learn strategies to keep your depression at bay or get to the root of a hurt which, once found, banishes that depression for good and all. But such discoveries, useful and liberating as they may be, are by-products of one central purpose which is to reassure you that despair need not be endured alone and that crises can be shared.

Winston Churchill famously described his depression as 'the black dog'. It is an appropriate description. Starkly terrifying yet terrifyingly ordinary, depression is an entity almost animal-like in its tenacity; one which will simply not let go when it has you in its grip. However, unpredictable beast that it is, it chooses, every now and then, to relax its jaws and to give you a moment's rest. But your relief is tainted because long experience has acquainted you with the dog's other sly characteristic. You know, for example, that, like some malevolent domestic familiar, it never really goes away. It merely moves to another part of the house, slinking around noiselessly, waiting by the kitchen door (or outside the bedroom or in the garden) ready to pounce when you least expect it. So even your brief moments of calm are infected by the knowledge (tinged with more than a little fear) that the beast will return.

But beasts can be tamed. Or contained. Or dealt with. Reassuring you of this is another aim of this book. What follows is ONE view of depression. It is not the *only* one. It is not one which every psychiatrist and clinician in the land may feel able to endorse. But it is one which many sufferers will recognise. It draws on the individual experiences of men and women in distress, on the wisdom acquired by some of the professionals who have treated them, and on the insights of some of the 23,000 Samaritans who have listened to them. It draws on forty years of training men and women to listen to cries of despair and to convince the despairing that someone genuinely cares about them. This may not seem much but through long experience The Samaritans have learnt that it means a great deal.

So often we hide our depression; we try to bury it deep where it will not infect anybody else. It is the guilty secret that we keep to ourselves out of shame or fear. We are simply not SUPPOSED to be depressed. Magazines and TV programmes reinforce that feeling daily. And if we *are* depressed it is our fault. It is the result of something we have done. Or not done. It is a punishment, our just desserts for being the imperfect person we ought not to be.

Mention this to any self-help group where depressives meet to share their experiences and you are immediately met with vigorous nods of recognition. 'Yes,' said Alice at one such group, 'that's just how it is. It's a sense of shame. I just feel ashamed to be feeling as I do. So I keep quiet.'

At the same group Ross, a retired engineer who has suffered from depression for most of his adult life, shared his experience of visiting an unsympathetic GP some forty years ago. 'I was almost thrown out of the surgery for wasting his time', he says, the trauma clearly as vivid now as it was then. 'He told me I had good parents, good health and good prospects and should be ashamed of myself for wasting his time. The fact that I was waking up every day thinking, "Oh, my God. Another day to live through" didn't register as strange in the slightest. The GP said he had countless other young men on his books who were REALLY ill so I should go away and count my blessings.'

The net result of such a thoughtless bedside manner was to send Ross deeper and deeper into what he calls 'the pit' (as so many do) leaving him positively frightened of ever raising the subject again with his family doctor.

Thankfully such reactions, whether born out of ignorance or intolerance, have largely disappeared as the clinical root of depressive illness has come to light, but even today a residual prejudice persists that it is somehow not appropriate to suffer from depression.

Consider this. You have a headache. What is the first thing you do – even before you reach for the aspirin? Answer? You tell someone. That is just the way it is. You say to everyone in the office, to everyone in the corridor, to everyone on the factory floor out loud and, in short, to anyone and everyone who will listen 'I've got a splitting headache'. Even as you are clutching your aching temples you are announcing to the world that you are in pain. It is so instinctive and so natural that you feel no shame, no guilt, and no embarrassment. Why should you? Everyone has had a headache and now you have one, too. The same applies to a broken arm, a swollen ankle, a bad back. People ask you how you're doing and you tell them the truth. It hurts.

Now compare that everyday experience with this – and you will not need a degree in psychology to spot the contrast. You wake up (but that is the wrong phrase because you have spent the whole night in a sweat barely able to close your eyes), you haul yourself out of bed with heavy lids and a heart filled with dread. You look out of the window onto a sunlit lawn and see only grey. The day offers no promise, no satisfaction, no way out of a feeling that has you in its grip. You are depressed. All pleasures have palled, all appetites have vanished. There is just an ache that will not go away. It's physical but it's not physical. But it hurts. Oh, how it hurts. If only SOMEONE out there knew how you were feeling. Knew the sheer heroic effort it needed just to put one foot in front of the other.

And then quite casually someone enquires, 'You're looking a bit rough. How are you feeling?' 'Fine', you say.

Wait a minute. Fine? Yes, fine, because for some reason that is how you are programmed to respond. Physical illness is neutral. Mental illness is judged. At least that is how you perceive things.

Imagine another situation. You trap your hand in the car door and people are instantly sympathetic. 'Ooh, that must have hurt', they say with genuine concern. But when you are feeling that death would be a more attractive proposition than even getting out of bed, when you are unable to face the day and tremble at the prospect of putting your head outside the door, a rather different reaction is likely to be provoked . . . along the lines of, 'Snap out of it. Pull yourself together'. The implication is clear: you must have done something to bring all this about. And so, to avoid judgement and the implied rebuke you say simply, when asked how you feel, 'I'm fine'.

Steve is 36 and a computer programmer. Like many sufferers he feels he has been depressed for as long as he can remember. But things came to a head some years ago when clinical depression was diagnosed. After consistent periods off work he now has his moods under control thanks to a mixture of medication, group therapy and sheer effort of will. This is how he describes the secrecy of depression: 'There's a big unwritten social rule which says if anyone asks you how you are don't tell them the truth. You can be about to jump under a bus but if anybody asks how you are, or enquires after your mental well-being in the most casual way, you just say automatically, "Oh, I'm fine".'

When we are *physically* unwell, letting others know is often the first thing we do. When *mentally* unwell, it is the last thing we contemplate.

Pretence is a strategy we have all deployed at one time or another in our lives. We have not dared to be honest with ourselves and with others. We have kept the mask in place while behind it we were crying. And no matter how wretched we were feeling it was somehow better to pretend to others that we felt OK. To do anything else would have been to admit to a terrible, shameful, guilty secret.

We see how fulfilled people are, how confident they are, how at ease with themselves. In a word, we see how happy they are. So *we* should not be depressed either. And, if we are, then there is something drastically wrong with us.

But the real world is not organised like that. It is not a case of 'us' and 'them'; we the desperate, they the light of heart. We are all in this together and though we may feel we are the only ones on the planet with such depression to bear there are others like us everywhere. If not, why, in 1994, did The Samaritans receive 3.75 million calls? Why did doctors and secretaries, builders and hairdressers, teachers and musicians (the list is endless) pick up the phone and share their troubles with them?

Given the sheer scale of the phenomenon of depression, there may be another reason why so many of us prefer to sweep it under the carpet with a casual 'you'll soon be out of it', or an equally peremptory 'give it a couple of days and it'll pass'. Perhaps the reason is that we are fearful of contagion.

Dennis, diagnosed manic depressive and, at 42, unable to hold down his job in public relations, has a theory. 'For a lot of people nowadays,' he says, 'the pace of life is so frenetic and the pressures of the rat race so extreme that they are on an emotional knife edge. They are more vulnerable than they care to admit in public. To be in contact with someone who has gone over the edge is to be face to face with that vulnerability and that makes them uneasy. They don't want to know.'

Ian, a local housing officer in his early 30s, puts it more bluntly. 'There are lots of people who'll offer you a shoulder to cry on. But they can't handle it if you don't get better pretty damned quick. They'll sympathise for a while until it gets a bit of a bore. Then it's a case of, "Right, you've had your five minutes. Now bugger off". 'People you thought were your friends come round less and less,' says Dennis. 'I had a circle of about thirty but as things got worse that number dwindled gradually until I now only see a couple.'

Nick is 41, a promising writer until severe, chronic depression left him unable to function properly. 'Depression has a kind of double meaning to it,' he says. 'People say they're depressed when they're just feeling low for a few days. But when you're clinically depressed it's far worse than that. It's a torment. At its depths I thought I'd died and gone to hell.' Nick is not alone. You are not alone. This book will remind you of that fact at every turn. It tries to look at each stage of depression – its approach, its onset, and its aftermath – and to offer practical advice at every step.

First it will help you to recognise the signs and symptoms of despairing behaviour, to spot the trigger points that are likely to provoke a downturn in your general level of mental and emotional well-being. These will be different for each individual but may well form a recognisable pattern which can be spotted in advance. On the twin principles of 'forewarned is forearmed' and 'better the devil you know . . .' you may then find yourself in a position to see the danger signs approaching and to take evasive or self-protective action.

Next, if a depression takes hold, the book will try to help you to see a way through it. To help you decide for yourself who you ought to see. Will the offer of a friendly shoulder to cry on get you through or are you looking for independent and dispassionate advice from a professional? Should you consult your GP, or a trained and recognised psychotherapist? Would prescribed medication from your family doctor help or is what you need a no-holds-barred, unashamed outpouring of feeling to a sympathetic stranger at the other end of a telephone? This book will try to help you decide on the best option.

Finally, this book points the way forward. It will help you to consider the future and enable you to make choices in your own life. Having confronted your demons and not run away from them in abject terror, you may be surprised to discover that you *are* capable of making choices which seemed impossible even days earlier. You may then be in a position to develop your own personal strategies for coping and to begin to plan for the future.

And, once again, you will not be alone. In the course of this book you will meet men and women like yourself who have chosen to tell their story on paper and to offer up their own case histories. A word about them first, though. They have not been suggested, selected, or approached by The Samaritans. To do so would be in breach of their strict principle of confidentiality. No one contacting The Samaritans need fear that his or her own experience will be made public or in any way discussed outside the confines of the telephone room – one on one. You call them; they listen. And there the conversation stops. It is a private relationship where caller and listener can feel secure.

Nor would The Samaritans presume to contact their callers at a subsequent date to ask them to talk about their lives in public. They are often contacted by the media with such requests and constantly turn them down. To approach clients in such a way – even with the guarantee of anonymity – would run counter to their philosophy. A caller is vulnerable and that vulnerability must be respected and guarded at all costs – both while the person is talking and after the receiver has been replaced.

The people who appear in the following pages fall into two categories: those belonging to a growing number of self-help groups who have invited me to attend their sessions, and those who have reacted to an advertisement in the press which asked simply whether anyone who had experienced depression would be willing to discuss their experiences anonymously. With their full permission and in the full knowledge that their stories might appear in this book, people who have gone through the depths of depression were then encouraged simply to talk.

Some of these conversations have been reproduced here to enable you to compare notes. Not surprisingly a proportion of those who replied to the advertisement had indeed contacted The Samaritans and it was left to the respondents themselves to decide how much or how little of their experience they wished to share.

Isabelle, a 30-year-old French woman living in Britain and a cook by trade, suffers from depression. I met her at a group therapy session and invited her to keep a diary of her moods. She agreed and has allowed me to publish here an extract from a 12-day period in her life. Twelve days during which the world went on its 'metalled ways of time past and time future'. But 12 days during which time stopped for Isabelle, during which there was only the eternal present of a pain with no beginning and no end.

Thursday 15 February 1996
Once again I couldn't be bothered to get up this morning. Felt awful and frightened. Stayed in bed all day feeling sorry for myself. There will be trouble at work again tomorrow. Tried not to think about it or anything else. Wanted to die but didn't have any energy to do anything about it.

Friday 16 February
Forced myself out of bed to go to work. I had been awake for hours anyway. Felt awful and out of place at work. Couldn't concentrate. Got a last warning. It probably won't be long before I'm out of a job. Don't even care any more. Saw the psychiatrist in the afternoon. He tried again to convince me to go back to hospital. No way! Got into that horrible panicky state and couldn't calm down. He drugged me and sent me home by ambulance. Slept for ages.

Saturday 17 February
am: I don't believe it! The alarm woke me up this morning. I slept all night! I felt rested and OK. The pains in my chest and stomach had gone. Went to work and coped better. Maybe I'll get better after all. I might beat this thing. A good night's sleep makes all the difference!

pm: Went to see L after work. Had a terrible argument and fight with him. I could have killed him! Felt very scared and panicky. Stole some sleeping tablets from him. Everything is hopeless. I am useless. I will never get better. Took all the pills hoping not to wake up. Went to sleep.

Sunday 18 February
Woke up at 1.40am because of a nightmare. The tablets didn't seem to have any effect. Had a terrible panic attack. Blacked out. Came to feeling very dizzy, drowsy, and very tearful. Couldn't stop crying. And wishing I was dead. Had all these thoughts in my head about killing myself. Phoned The Samaritans. Talked it over for nearly three hours. Felt a bit better and completely exhausted and afraid to go to sleep.

Started wandering round the flat aimlessly. My head was hurting as if I had a hangover. Had a bath and managed to relax a bit. Went to bed and fell asleep immediately.

Monday 19 February
Woke up in panicky state because of a nightmare. It was 2.20am. Couldn't get back to sleep and felt very low. Is this ever going to end? Turned the TV on and flicked through the channels without watching anything. Turned off the sound and kept staring at the screen until it was time to get up. Didn't want to. I was feeling so weary. Dragged myself to work. Couldn't get into it and kept cutting or burning myself. At last the day was over. Had a bath and fell asleep in it. I hate that! I was very cold when I woke up. Went to bed but couldn't sleep.

Tuesday 20 February
It has been a very bad night and an awful day. It was gone 1.00am when I eventually went to sleep. Woke up around 2.30 because of another horrible nightmare. Got into a panicky state again and was very frightened. Couldn't get back to sleep and kept tossing and turning. Felt very alone and restless. Wanted to get up but it was too cold. Tried reading. No use. My lack of concentration is getting worse if that's possible. Put the telly on. Turned it off. I was feeling very down and sorry for myself. Fell asleep around 5.00am. Couldn't get up at 6. The next thing I knew it was 10.20am and the phone was ringing. It was work. That's it; I've lost my job again. I am such a failure. I will never get anywhere. I burst into tears, took some tablets and got very drunk hoping to knock myself out. Fell asleep. Woke up and was as sick as a dog. It was awful. I wanted to die. Went back to sleep.

Wednesday 21 February
Woke up again in the middle of the night. My body was hurting all over and I had a terrible hangover. Didn't have any energy whatsoever. Couldn't even put the light on and thinking was too hard and too painful. So I just lay in bed very still for hours. Fell asleep, woke up, slept again on and off all day long. I was totally drained, even too tired to think or move a muscle. Slowly towards the evening my ability to think came back and, with it, a very strong feeling of despair. I was so alone I couldn't stand it. So I phoned The Samaritans. It helped a lot. I felt at peace within myself and was able to go to sleep.

Thursday 22 February
Now that was the best night I've had in ages. I woke just after 11.00am and felt fine. Stayed in bed a bit longer, enjoying that rare feeling of well-being. I was trying to sort my life out in my head. It seemed I could resume the fight and I wanted to recover. So I got up and went out to start looking for another job. I felt confident I could handle it better this time. I asked for three application forms over the phone and secured an interview for tomorrow. I had the feeling that I had achieved something for once. Went to bed in a good mood.

Friday 23 February
Woke up just before 4.00am and started to worry about the job interview. Tried to prepare myself for it. Went back to sleep around 7.00am and woke up at 11 feeling OK but a bit nervous. At least I had something to get up for. I think the interview went pretty well. Should know early next week. Replied to two more ads.

Saturday 24 February
Woke up in a panic at 3.10am. I don't even know why. Everything seemed gloomy and I felt pretty low. Was wondering about the meaning of life and it doesn't seem worth living. Went back to sleep ages later and woke up at 9.25 with a nightmare. Didn't panic this time and I wasn't feeling too bad. Had a bath and could relax a little. Should have gone out in the evening but I didn't feel up to it so I stayed in.

Sunday 25 February
Once again I woke up in the early hours with a nightmare and once again I was panicking. I hate that awful feeling of suffocation which takes ages to release its hold of me. Tossed and turned for hours. Feeling very down eventually I gave in and picked up the phone. I'm calling The Samaritans more and more often these days. Things have really gone out of control. Forced myself out of bed just before my first student came [Isabelle gives French tuition]. Taught for three hours but couldn't concentrate. That really gets to me. I feel as if I'm cheating these youngsters and that's horrible. Went straight back to bed afterwards and stayed there feeling sorry for myself for the rest of the day.

Monday 26 February
Didn't sleep at all last night. I was feeling so restless. I

couldn't even keep still. Kept getting up to wander round the flat aimlessly. Went for a long walk some time between 2 and 3. Got lost. Panicked, blacked out and ended up in hospital. They drugged me and let me sleep it off before sending me home. I'm sure the psychiatrist is going to hear about it. There is trouble ahead. Once home I went to bed and slept most of the day until it was time to teach. Managed two hours of it and went back to bed completely worn out.

Such an honest testimony hints at what it is really like down there in the depths. Merely to get up out of bed requires a monumental effort. Merely to go on needs a reservoir of courage deeper than most of us possess.

The purpose of including first person testimonies like this is simple: to persuade those who are depressed that where they are now others have gone before – and that, despite their suffering, many have emerged from the shadows into the sunlight once again.

* * *

When faced with another's depression people often have a reaction at first sight quite different from the judgemental – but it is invariably just as unhelpful. It seems like compassion but it isn't. They will put a metaphorical arm round the sufferer's shoulder and say, 'Cheer up. I know how you feel'. The facts are these: (a) you can't and (b) they don't.

Unlike them, this book does not set out to give glib advice in the expectation that everything will turn out just fine. It may not. And some things may simply have to be endured with great fortitude. But this book is based on the conviction all *ultimately* need not be gloom.

Why? Because people who were once depressed have said so. On the strength of their testimony and with the help of professionals who have treated them, this book dares to say hesitantly, in the words of the 14th-century mystic, Mother Julian of Norwich (herself no stranger to sickness, depressions, visions, and voices), that 'all shall be well and all manner of things shall be well'.

Judge for yourself and take it a page at a time.

1

No End To Experience: Recognising Depression

'Depression is a life-threatening illness'. Such is Kathy's verdict on a condition which cut short her career as an infant school teacher, left her fearful and uncertain, accompanied her in and out of mental hospitals, and prompted her to write persistent, nagging letters to the social services department in an endless and unspecified complaint against something or other.

Depression has taken her to the verge of alcoholism and haunts her still. She has it under control, she thinks, but it is never far away. For the moment she has her life on a reasonable course, studying at college once again at the age of 40. But she treats her apparent equanimity with caution. At any moment the black dog could pounce. It knows where she lives.

James, too, has had his own strategy for survival. He has learnt to spot the pattern of his depression and to be prepared for it when it strikes. At its worst it would affect him for ten months at a time but give him respite for a few precious weeks. These he would enjoy while he could, using them as sustenance to keep him going during the hard times ahead. And they *were* hard.

'I felt as if I was dead', he says with a sigh of resignation but not defeat. 'I lay in bed all day long staring at the ceiling, imprisoned by my own thoughts. I had exactly the same menu every day. Brown bread, sardines, butter, and milk. The butter went on the bread and the sardines went on the butter. And that was it for months on end.'

That should not, in theory, happen to a Sandhurst-trained former Captain in the Royal Engineers who, in Civvy Street, had bought and successfully managed two supermarkets. But it did. Now, with a 'cocktail' of drugs, he says he has the condition under control though it has exacted a terrible price. 'The only thing I knew was that it would come to an end in time and that I would get a good patch lasting a few weeks. So what I would do was to trade off the few weeks against the months.'

These two examples are not unique but they are at the extreme end of the spectrum of depression. At the other is the vague feeling of things being rather flat, a feeling of 'being low', 'down in the dumps', or 'having a bad day'. The problem in putting a name to whatever sensation of unease you are experiencing at any one time is that the spectrum is as wide as experience itself.

An advertising firm once coined the phrase, 'Hard to define. Easy to recognise'. The copywriters doubtless had something far more glamorous than depression in mind but their skill in creating so useful a term is to be commended. Not for nothing is depression, that most familiar yet intractable of mental conditions, called 'the common cold of psychiatric medicine'.

Medical fashions come and go and words which were once thought helpful cease to be used as new insights into mental illness are gained. For all that, certain broad categories have been identified over the years and they may not yet fully have outlived their usefulness.

Types of depression

Depression encompasses an enormous range of emotional states, not all of them classifiable as illnesses. Look at what is happening at any given moment in a person's life and there will be quite understandable reasons why someone is feeling low (or worse). Such states have often been called 'reactive' or 'environmental' or, more academically, 'exogenous' – meaning 'coming from the outside'.

In such a state a patient will have been propelled into depression by an event or series of events which has triggered a lowering of his or her mood. A list of significant life-changing events has been compiled by observers of these phenomena and includes, at one extreme, bereavement and, further down the scale of severity, such things as moving house or changing jobs.

More detail follows later but, for now, the principle is clear.

Life experiences exact a price. We do not go through life untouched by it – although some people, wishing things were otherwise, may be tempted to enlist elaborate means to keep reality at bay. And success may ultimately prove two edged: these people may succeed in erecting such defences against this rough, rude, and mysterious thing we call life that they manage to keep its joys at arm's length as well as its pains.

But a depressed person does not have the luxury of such philosophical reflection. For when life's pains – the death of a child or a parent, a suicide in the family, the loss of a limb, divorce, unemployment, homelessness or whatever – are visited on us (as they are on someone somewhere every second of every day) we find it very difficult to look on the bright side of things. For the moment there is only one side to consider; and that can look very black indeed.

But on such occasions, when depression does ensue, at least it has the merit of comprehensibility. Reactive depression, you *could* say (though admittedly when you are depressed you would have a hard time actually *saying* it) is a thoroughly natural response to what the world has thrown at you.

By contrast, the second category of depression, which has been termed 'endogenous' or 'coming from within', is a much more problematic condition to explain. In broad terms doctors ascribe this to a chemical or electrical imbalance in the make-up of the brain, an imbalance which physical intervention in the form of medication or electro-convulsive therapy (ECT) may be able to put right.

Now, a crash course in neuro-physiology is a dangerous undertaking and not one which anyone outside the medical field should embark on lightly. Indeed it is far beyond the remit of this book to explain either the detailed workings of the human brain or the current state of neurological research which anyway is in a constant state of evolution.

However, this is how consultant psychiatrist, Sally Pidd, explains things in shorthand to her patients on those occasions when she is prescribing them anti-depressants. She compares the brain to a battery which, to function properly, needs a conducting fluid of some kind to bridge the gap between two poles. 'What seems to be the case in depression is that there isn't enough of the transmitter substance between the interconnecting neurons of the brain. When an electrical impulse gets to the end of a neuron a chemical is released which bridges the gap to the next neuron. What anti-depressants do is to concentrate on that gap.'

It sounds simple enough. And to some degree it is. 'The way in which anti-depressants work,' she says, 'is really quite well known.' But, and it's a big but, she adds, 'What people don't know is WHY this process should make people depressed in the first place. People will often say to me, "Can't you do a test to see whether I'm properly topped up?" And the answer is no. Even to call these conductors "fluids" is misleading. They are there in such microscopic levels that we don't really have a comparison in the ordinary everyday world. In theory it seems to be a very reasonable question as to why we don't have a marker for depression. But the plain fact is, we don't.'

Endogenous depression sneaks up on you unawares. A thought can provoke it, a sight, a sound, a smell can trigger it and transform a hitherto good mood into something which leaves you low for the day. Or for the week. If we could predict when such a mood would strike we would be better able to cope with it when it does. But the fact is that most of the time we simply don't know why we should be prey to such mood change.

My eight-year-old son gave me an insight into the phenomenon when he remarked that he did not always like the sunlight.

'Why not?' I asked.

'Well, sometimes it doesn't look nice. It makes me sad.'

'How do you mean?' I continued casually.

'Well, you know when we go to Jimmy's Cafe [an occasional Saturday treat when the two of us have breakfast out] sometimes the sun shines on the wall by Sainsbury's and I feel a bit sad.'

'Why's that, do you think?'

'Well, it reminds me of Granny's funeral.'

'Was that what the light looked like then?'

'Yes.'

'You cried when Granny died, didn't you?'

'Yes.'

'It was very sad, wasn't it.'

'Yes.'

'No wonder you feel a bit sad when anything reminds you of it again. Like that wall for instance.'

'Dad?'

'Yes?'

'When are we going swimming?'

The moment of minor crisis had passed and we were once again in the realm of planning our day's events. But I have no doubt that in years to come, when my son is on a beach in Cornwall, or playing cricket in a team, or laughing with his girl-friend on a carefree summer's holiday, or loading his children into the car for a trip to the coast, he will look up and see a patch of light that momentarily and inexplicably drains things of all their colour.

He will see the light just as it struck Sainsbury's wall near Jimmy's Cafe all those years ago. And though he will have for-gotten the circumstances of granny's funeral he will look up and catch an indefinable intensity of light that takes him back to a chilly cemetery, to silent, grieving adults, and to that moment when he felt alone with his tears. And no one will have the power to make him 'snap out of it'. Because no one registered that unrepeatable moment in quite the same way as he did. And the help I, his loving father, can offer is limited.

The next time I passed Jimmy's Cafe I made a special point of looking at the wall. To me, of course, it was just another wall. And the light? Well, it was just sunlight. Nothing special – *as far as I could see*. And if in the future he tells me he is feeling sad or depressed I shall think twice before saying in return, 'Yes, John, I know how you feel'. I don't.

This, of course, is a minor experience but it illustrates a general principle – that so often the causes of depression are mysterious. One minute we can be feeling fine and the next we are feeling inexplicably miserable. That is why this whole area is full of complexity and ambivalence.

That the roots of depression are chemical, that this deficient chemistry is inherited, that it is in our genes and that individuals must simply accept that they have a greater or lesser genetic predisposition to it is just one school of thought. Others say that the roots are traceable to infant and childhood experiences, to early trauma and bad parenting (though the latter may not be synonymous with having bad parents who may in good conscience and with flawed affection have done many of the wrong things for all the right reasons). Others say that depression is a form of repressed anger. And, indeed, it is easy to believe that the powerlessness, the unexpressed sense of outrage, and the sheer volume of suppressed rage in the face of, say, childhood sexual abuse or emotional cruelty can turn in on themselves only to come out again, much later in life, in the form of depression.

So, there are many theories and it is likely that all of them contain a measure of truth. It is equally likely that depression is often a combination of all the above. That said, doctors and researchers have isolated certain conditions which can, to some degree, be explained and which can, to a corresponding degree, be treated successfully. Stand by for a spot of jargon.

Unipolar affective disorder

This is what the layperson might reasonably call the standard form of depression – though differences in severity make it different for each individual. It can be classified as mild, moderate, or severe, but, even at its mildest, it is several notches up from just feeling under the weather. It affects one's performance at work and one's personality at home. Clinical depression of this type changes the pattern of one's life to an uncomfortable degree and can be identified by certain symptoms. The most common are:

Fatigue and sleep disorder

The tiredness is not the healthy variety that follows a long walk, or a game of tennis. It is heavy, persistent and inexplicable. What is more, it is not removed by sleep which sometimes seems to induce even greater lethargy. The patterns of sleep become perverse. You go to bed and cannot sleep at all so prowl the house until three in the morning. You get to sleep eventually but wake in the night checking the clock at regular intervals. Whatever pattern you fall into you feel that you have never had a 'good' night's sleep and wake up invariably tired. Some, by contrast, will sleep all day lacking the energy to get up at all.

Lack of motivation

Everything is too much trouble. Even the simplest tasks seem like major enterprises requiring enormous reserves of strength and will-power. Washing dishes, tidying the garage, or organising your paperwork all seem like Everests to climb.

Poor concentration

Focusing your attention on anything for any sustained amount of time becomes increasingly difficult. You scan newspapers and magazines from cover to cover but find it hard to read an article to the end. Sitting down and addressing one task requires a real effort of will. You abandon projects half-way through, leave dressmaking projects unfinished or the lawn half mown. The easiest of jobs take twice the amount of time they used to. You seem uncharacteristically careless. When using the word processor you make more than the usual number of basic typing errors; when changing the car battery you repeatedly drop the spanner or select the wrong bolts. People give you directions and you fail to absorb the information. You stare at a pile of change in your hand and, for the life of you, cannot assemble the right coins for a carton of milk.

Forgetfulness

You come into the room and find yourself at a loss to know what you came for. You put down your keys and spend ten minutes trying to retrieve them. Then you go out minus your overcoat. Dental appointments are missed. Letters are unanswered.

Appetite disorder and weight fluctuation

You find yourself overeating even though you are not hungry. You eat sweet or stodgy foods for the sake of the comfort they bring. As a consequence you put on weight uncharacteristically. Or you go to the other extreme and find that you lack all interest in food. Your appetite and your weight decrease abnormally.

Feelings of inadequacy

You feel you are not up to the demands of the job you have been doing for years. That you are not a worthy partner in a relationship. Your self-esteem and your self-confidence take a nosedive for no apparent reason. You feel your contribution to a project or a discussion will be worthless so you decide not to contribute. Situations get on top of you; bills pile up, clothes stay unironed, books remain unread. You feel guilty for the way you are but powerless to change things.

Loss of vitality

All the things that used to make you happy don't any more. Going for a cycle ride or for a walk in the park have simply lost their appeal. The cinema, the theatre, football matches, the television or whatever lack all interest or attraction. Your interest in sex declines. The world looks blank.

Minor ailments

You are assailed by an apparently never-ending series of aches and pains. Colds recur or will not clear up. A cough or a sore throat plagues you constantly. You seem to get headaches and toothaches all the time. What's more, you are beset by the gnawing fear that these minor ailments are a sign of serious illness – but you do nothing about them with the result that your anxiety increases.

Irrational fear

For no obvious reason you feel anxious and afraid. The world seems a dangerous and a sinister place with all manner of traps to ensnare you. You see only the negative aspects of life while the positive things have lost all power to cheer you. You have a pessimistic view of the future and become unreasonably affected by thoughts of nuclear catastrophe, global warming, environmental pollution, cruelty to animals and so on. You feel hypersensitive and vulnerable and pass on that vulnerability to your family. You become over-protective of your children.

Confusion

You cannot express yourself as fluently as before. You cannot put thoughts into words or describe emotional states. You frequently make yourself misunderstood or find it hard to talk naturally to strangers and friends alike.

Intolerance

The children's high spirits set you on edge. You are angry or impatient at the slightest of things. Noises and bright lights upset you. Your normal tolerance levels slip and your emotional defences are down. You are often tearful for no obvious reason or you well up at the slightest provocation – a sentimental tune, a scene in a TV soap, news reports of war and starvation and so on.

Self-hatred

You have a feeling of not being at ease with yourself, not being right in your own skin. You feel you are bad, not nice to know, sinful, ugly. You feel unloved and unlovable – which is not surprising given the feelings you have towards yourself. You do not love yourself so is it surprising that you believe no one else does either?

Self-harm

At the back of your mind you have vague thoughts of hurting yourself or punishing yourself for some unstated failing or misdemeanour. You may already have committed minor acts of self-harm like drawing a razor blade across your skin while in the bath or cutting yourself with knives.

Suicidal thoughts

You have positive and increasingly focused thoughts on the business of taking your own life. You think about methods and imagine possible scenarios. You consider the practicalities of accumulating pills, or of buying a gun, or of leaping off a high building. You indulge in a bleak and restricted view of your own role in the world's affairs and give in to a sense of self-pity at your own predicament (which you may feel is entirely justified).

Registering one or more of the above symptoms need not indicate clinical depression. Indeed, given the right set of circumstances, all of us have probably displayed, at one time or another in our lives, more than one of them (with the arguable exception of suicidal thoughts). It is when the symptoms begin to build up and crowd in that alarm bells should start to ring.

During a mild depression, sufferers have relatively little difficulty in coping with the symptoms. They will be uncomfortable but not debilitating. Either the symptoms are comparatively slight or they are severe but last only a short space of time and recur infrequently if at all.

When a combination of symptoms conspires to interfere with what we might loosely call normal life then it is likely that an individual will be suffering from an attack of moderate depression. Things may not have reached such a pitch that a person cannot make it into school, university or work but it is common, at this stage of the condition, for him or her to find it increasingly difficult to do the task in hand. Normal life (and we each know what we mean by this) is becoming progressively hard to sustain. It is at this point that we may find it advisable to seek advice or practical help.

It is, however, precisely at this point that a proportion of people (and, it has to be said, particularly men) refuse to seek such help. To do so, for some, is a sign of weakness; for others, as described earlier, it is a badge of shame. So they let things slide. This can be dangerous. Because if outside circumstance or inner chemistry is not addressed then the depression may move imperceptibly to a higher level of severity. As if caught in an advancing tide those susceptible to such mood disorders can then find themselves engulfed in successive waves of unpleasant and possibly destructive feelings.

Severe depression is often likened to a prison from which there is no escape; a tunnel which admits no light; a nightmare from which there is no awakening.

> ❛It was absolute hell on earth. I was overwhelmed with a sense of total uselessness. I had no communication with my wife, no communication with my children. People came to the door and I'd ignore them. I didn't want anyone to enter into my pain or to increase it. I used to go physically cold inside while I was blocking everything and everyone out. There was just me and this pain. And nothing else. ❜
>
> *Paul, 53, former vicar*

> ❛It's horrible. I can't concentrate on anything. I feel like cry-ing all the time. I can't sleep and when I do I wake up in the middle of the night with nightmares. I have blackouts and anxiety attacks and basically I want to be on my own. ❜
>
> *Isabelle, 30, cook*

Pits, tunnels, and prisons are difficult to get out of. So, too, is severe depression. To use another analogy it is like a black hole in deep space. Once inside it, the pull of its gravitational mass is so intense as to prevent anything from escaping. No light gets in; nothing gets out. The darkness entombs all. Severe depression, so people will tell you, feels just like that. And very possibly a bit worse.

So intense is the pain – beyond all our individual imaginings – that some sufferers take their own lives. Whether coolly, rationally, and deliberately or whether on a whim while the balance of the mind is beyond all external control, we shall never know. All we can say with some degree of certainty is that the emotional vacuum at the core of one human being's consciousness was so great as to render existence impossible. And so the darkness claims another victim.

But take heart. The analogy of the black hole is flawed. Otherwise how could so many have emerged from it, at enormous cost to themselves, to tell their stories? Even so, the fact remains that those in the grip of a deep depression will find self-help increasingly difficult (if not absolutely impossible). The more severe the condition the less able the sufferer will be to do anything about it. And the less able the person is to fight back the more severe the depression may become. That is why early action is advised. Better that than a slow slide down a decidedly vicious spiral.

Bipolar affective disorder

This is sometimes known as 'manic depression' where mood oscillates between unnatural highs and equally alarming lows as if one's emotions were constantly on a see-saw. Excessive energy and elation give way to lethargy and despair and while the sufferer tends to feel better while the mania is in the ascendant his or her family will often find the behaviour rather troubling.

It may, for example, be a distinct source of embarrassment to see a father or a mother taking an excessive or immoderate interest in sexual flirtatiousness; it will almost certainly be destructive of familial harmony to see a member embarking on a series of wild affairs, or arguably worse still, to stand helplessly by as mother or father gives everything up in the pursuit of an impossible love object. Financial stability can be threatened when the breadwinner, in a reckless, manic phase, takes to gambling the housekeeping on the lottery or scratchcards. Even a person's physical safety will be imperilled should the mania induce an unreasonable passion for fast driving or dangerous sports. Even talking non-stop to complete strangers on a train is not without its hazards.

As Kathy puts it:

❝ The manic phase is a totally false sense of elation. It's not true happiness. I've known people who play Wagner on the record player all night long. I used to run baths all the time. And then go out because I couldn't stay in one place. I just had to get out of the house because I felt so restless. I was aware that I was behaving irrationally but there was nothing I could do about it. ❞

Or Dennis:

❝ I just wasn't sleeping. I was on the go all the time. Night and day. I worked out once that over a period of 20 days I had 54 hours' sleep. And most of that was taken in a solid block. I might have had three days when I slept for ten hours a day and another three when I didn't sleep at all. I just used to wander about all night going to all-night snooker clubs and stuff. ❞

As a young trainee officer James was aware of similar mood swings which, in his case, were not always harmful. On the contrary he could turn them to positive advantage. 'I'm of below-average height,' he says. 'But when I used to play rackets, one of the fastest sports around, I used to wipe the floor with the opposition, even though they were a good few inches taller. I had great pace. On a route march I would usually be the smallest but I'd end up carrying four rifles and still coming home first. That's what manic depressives can do.'

Manic depression does, however, respond to treatment and with the right medication the highs and the lows can be controlled – though not always to an individual's satisfaction, as James has noticed within the self-help group he runs in South London. 'The drug Lithium helps even out the highs and the lows,' he says, 'but we had a person within the group who gave it up because he found that it took away his flair for writing music. So he accepted his lows because his highs were all the better for it.'

The ambivalence of such a condition is clear. Provided the symptoms are neither unwanted, dangerous, threatening, or criminal there may be a very compelling case for saying that living with the sickness is better than undergoing the cure. Such decisions, however, are best arrived at in collaboration with all those affected. A sufferer's partner, for example, may well appreciate the heightened sense of joy the sufferer feels at certain moments in the mood cycle but is only too keenly aware of the corresponding cold plunge into despondency when the downturn kicks in.

Seasonal affective disorder

It seems quite reasonable to assume that most people, given the choice, would prefer long summer days filled with sunshine rather than a short few hours of winter daylight. We might prefer them but would we necessarily get depressed if deprived of them? The fact is that most of us would not. We have learnt to live with the cycle of the seasons and positively welcome some of the by-products of autumn and winter. Cosy evenings round the fire with the curtains drawn against the December darkness can be positively savoured. And anyone living in a region where the temperature constantly hovered in the 70s and the sun stubbornly refused to set would undoubtedly miss out on a real pleasure.

Some people, however, suffer from positive symptoms of depression when the hours of daylight are restricted. Experiments (and individual experiences) show that in some sufferers emotional moods are lowered in direct proportion to the decline of daylight hours. Correspondingly, spirits can be raised after a period of exposure even to artificial light.

To be classified as someone suffering from SAD (as it is known) there has to be evidence that the depression occurs in recognisable cycles which begin, in England at least, sometime around September and end sometime around April. One plan of action, if circumstances and finances permit, is of course to take to sunnier climes when the nights begin to pull in. Failing that, if the depression is not too severe, you can try some of the self-help measures described later in the book. A recognised association exists to give further information to those who think they may be suffering from the condition.

Postnatal depression

Twice as many women as men are reckoned to suffer from depression – though it has been argued that this is because men have a tendency to keep their emotions to themselves and to suffer silently. Statistics notwithstanding, this is one category of depression that men are spared – although its effects will often have real consequences for the family, and therefore, for the husband or partner.

The maelstrom of hormonal activity that is triggered in a woman's body at the time of childbirth is, has been, and will continue to be the subject of clinical research for as long as medicine is practised. It is fruitless, then, in so general a book to speculate on the precise role of the hormones in inducing depression at such a complex moment in the life cycle of a woman. Suffice to say they *do* have a role to play.

Against this background, however, other psychological factors are brought into play. The joy at 'bringing new life into the world' is not unalloyed. The father might already have disappeared from the scene leaving the mother worried at how she is to bring up the baby alone once life has settled down to normal once more. Then again, the father may be all too solidly on the scene, laying down the law in the household, demanding that his every need be met by the mother who now has *another* child on her hands. Not to mention the reality, in certain unhappy households, of domestic violence.

These are reasons enough in themselves to get depressed – despite (whatever anybody says) that radiant, seraphic face glowing in the cot beside the hospital bed. Most (men) who are inclined to draw attention to the cute little face in the knitted bonnet carefully avoid reference to the other bits lower down the mattress, the messier bits that are the focus for sheer hard work as opposed to passive wonderment. Pure resentment that life will not be instantly transformed in some magical way by the miracle of birth can be enough in itself to induce depression. After nine long months of sickness, backache, and discomfort comes the dawning revelation that the real hard work is about to begin. After three cosseted days in hospital, another period of selfless endeavour soon gets under way – and this time its length is to be measured in years.

Let's face it. It's enough to make anyone depressed. This may be exaggeration to make a point. But the point remains. In the experience of many women this is a reality every bit the equal of the deep satisfaction of motherhood. But other feelings come into the picture, too. And although it seems shameful even to think it, with birth comes a kind of death. The death, for some women, of their independent selves; the feeling that all they might have achieved through study or hard work is now at an end. Their freedom is lost for 18 years and more, and with it their own separate identity. A precious part of them has died and, yes, the beloved child will more than compensate but, they ask, 'Will someone out there please just acknowledge that something has been sacrificed to make all this possible?'

Then again, which some may find arguably more shameful still, there is a feeling that the mother's sexual attractiveness has gone, that the bloom of youth has faded to be replaced by asexual maternity. Grannies can be glamorous in holiday-camp parades. But can mums ever really be sexy again? The answer, of course, is a resounding 'yes' but many will find it very difficult to be persuaded in the immediate aftermath of what is a traumatic experience by *any* standards.

When all the questions and all the doubts have been rehearsed in the solitude of the maternity ward a kind of sadness can intrude. And this in turn can harden into depression. This may last only a few days but it is as real as the bootees and the furry animals; as real as the household to which the mother and the proud father cautiously return. But what is particularly bewildering about this extremely common condition (and it applies equally well to depression itself) is that sometimes *no* reason can be found to explain it.

None of the above circumstances may apply and a woman may still feel depressed and at a loss to know why her mood has taken a dive. She knows full well that she was looking forward to the baby's birth with a sense of pleasurable anticipation. She has a loving and supportive husband or partner who will share the duties and responsibilities equally. And yet still she feels depressed. 'What's wrong?' she wonders gloomily, 'it must be me.' She looks at the baby and sees a perfectly beautiful child but cannot bring herself to shake off this heavy feeling of despondency. So she concludes, wrongly, that she is at fault, that she is somehow not cut out for motherhood, and not like all those cheerful 'normal' mothers surrounding her.

Postnatal depression (PND) may last for only a few days (though, while it lasts, it is real enough) or it may continue for months with all the symptoms of generalised depression – disrupted sleep, bone-weary tiredness, eating disorders. On top of it all there is a wretched feeling that life has lost its attractions, that nothing seems carefree anymore. There is no fun in life. Sometimes, it seems, nothing to make life worth living at all.

It is also a time when anxiety can strike. A mother may be constantly fretting that the baby is not developing as it should; she will be disproportionately alarmed at the slightest rash or the slightest cough. Should its eyes be like that? Is it eating enough? Should I leave it alone? She constantly checks the baby in the cot, getting up from the bed six or more times a night to check that it is still breathing. After all she has read about cot death she fears that her baby will be its next victim. These are all symptoms of heightened anxiety which is common among those in the grip of PND.

That anxiety, however, may manifest itself in other ways. Instead of feeling overly protective a mother may feel unnaturally cold and distant. She does not want to do the baby any actual harm but she feels indifferent and removed, as though her maternal feelings have been cut off at the roots. All this can lead her to make excessive demands on her health visitor or GP, who will be well placed to offer her the desperate reassurance she seeks. Her moods, however, can cause stress in the home as she inevitably draws the father into her own anxiety, sometimes pleading with him to stay with her instead of going off to work. At times like this he needs to be told that such reactions are quite common.

Being told about the condition is undoubtedly helpful. More helpful still is to be told what can be done about it. The first thing, as always, is recognition. Many mothers simply do not know they have PND and assume that this is motherhood so they had better get used to it. Or they know that *something* is wrong but are too ashamed to admit it. Talking to a midwife or health visitor is vital. After all they have seen this before and can reassure you that you are not an oddity. The next stage may be a visit to the GP who may, if the condition is particularly severe, prescribe a course of medication.

As part of its Defeat Depression Campaign, the Royal Colleges of Psychiatrists and GPs have produced a pamphlet on all aspects of PND and they have concluded that PND can be prevented. Prevention, they say, takes three forms: stopping it from happening in the first place, nipping it in the bud, and preventing things from getting worse. While stopping short of waving a magic wand they go on to suggest certain common-sense principles which could be effective.

What not to do

- Don't try to be a superwoman. If you are in full-time employment try to reduce your commitments during pregnancy. Go easy on yourself at work and put your feet up at lunchtime.
- Don't move house (if you can help it) while you are pregnant or until the baby is six months old.
- Don't blame yourself or your partner. Natural irritability on both sides can lead to quarrels but having a go at each other weakens a relationship when it needs to be at its strongest.
- Don't be afraid to ask for help when you need it.

What to do

- Identify someone in whom you can confide. It may be a relative, a friend, or your next-door neighbour. Feel at ease communicating your feelings rather than bottling them up.
- Go to antenatal classes and take your partner with you.
- Take every opportunity of getting rest once the baby has arrived.
- Eat healthily.

- Have fun with your partner. Make space for yourselves. Find a baby-sitter and go out for a meal or a drink or to the cinema.
- Let yourself and your partner be intimate. Even if you are not ready for sex, kiss and cuddle one another.

The message is a positive one. Some combination of informal talk, professional counselling, support and medication will make a big difference and will speed up the process of eventual recovery.

Puerperal psychosis

An altogether different state from postnatal depression, a million miles away from the baby blues, this is the most severe form of depression attending the experience of childbirth. Consultant psychiatrist, Dr Sally Pidd, has had experience of working with the women (somewhere in the region of one in 500 new mothers) who have developed the condition – usually in the first two weeks after giving birth. 'Whereas one in ten women usually suffers from postnatal depression,' she says, 'which often comes on some weeks after they've had the baby and is frequently associated with tiredness, poor concentration, not coping, weepiness, generally feeling low and so on, women with PND are still quite in touch with reality.'

The distinguishing feature of psychosis is its tendency to take the sufferer beyond the bounds of ordinary experience into a realm which has ceased to operate according to the laws of what we would call external reality. It is a state prey to internal voices and hallucinations where sufferers claim to be hearing messages from higher beings (notably from God) instructing them to behave in dramatic ways. As Dr Pidd puts it, 'Sufferers will not only feel depressed and worthless, which quite a lot of people feel. They may say that their insides have withered – physically dried up within them – and this is preventing them from eating or functioning properly or whatever.'

Transfer such delusions to the recovery ward and the potential for extreme behaviour is clear. Some mothers will display all

the signs of (treatable) psychiatric illness, often becoming confused and disorientated, with feelings of antipathy towards the
baby that can escalate into actual (and, in tragic cases, successful) attempts on the baby's life. They may think the baby is not
theirs at all, that theirs has been spirited away and replaced by
something that does not belong to them; they may feel that the
baby is an evil presence (sometimes the devil incarnate) and *in
extremis* will take their own life with that of their baby. Such
instances may be rare but documentary evidence shows that
they exist. And they stem, to a greater or lesser degree, from this
baffling condition we call depression. Meanwhile we scratch our
heads and ask the persistent and tantalising question: why?

It is clear that anyone who convincingly supplies an answer
will find the world's doctors, psychiatrists, and pharmacologists
– not to mention its philosophers, novelists, and poets – beating
a path to their door. But until that riddle has been successfully
solved depression will merely have to be accepted for what it is.
An immensely complex phenomenon of our human existence,
unpredictable but occasionally understandable; agonising but
ultimately treatable.

2

The Next Step

So, you have looked down the list of symptoms and concluded that more than a couple apply to you. Now you have corroboration of what you had suspected all along; that you are depressed. Congratulations, for the second time. It may not feel like it at the time but, armed with knowledge and recognition, you are now on the path towards treatment. And, by extension, some way along the road to recovery.

The fact is that many people do NOT realise that they are depressed at all and turn up at their doctor's surgery with signs of some other physical ailment which they assume is totally unrelated to the nagging, debilitating mental condition which somehow does not seem worth mentioning or which, as we saw before, they dare not bring up out of weakness, fear, or shame.

> ❮ The first time I actually spoke to a doctor about things I didn't really know what depression was. I had just been feeling in a state of total confusion. I thought I was going mad. It was an extreme version of standing in the kitchen wondering what you'd come in for. I couldn't think straight. I kept putting things down and forgetting what I'd done with them. I forgot my own middle name at one stage which is quite ridiculous. My problem was that I had always been a great one for saying, "Ho, ho, ho. I'm all right really. Yes, I've been feeling suicidal for months but I'm fine". And then I had to admit, "I'm not fine at all". It's a bit like not wanting to go to the doctor's in case they find something wrong with you. So you sit tight and hope it will go away. And in my case it didn't. ❯
>
> *Steve, 36, telephone engineer*

There are many people who take Steve's course of action and make an appointment with their GP on the understanding that they have an essentially physical complaint that the doctor can put right; the cold that has lingered for six months, the insomnia, the fatigue at work, the diminishing sex drive that has left a partner feeling bewildered and unloved, even the sprained ankle or the broken arm. These are simple physical problems, the patient reasons, that a prescription will put right; nothing to do with (the voice now trailing to a whisper) mental illness.

That is not necessarily how the GP will view things, however, as Dr André Tylee knows from long experience. The first thing he has to do (and others like him who have made depression a specialism) is to look behind the immediate symptoms and, by focused questioning, decide whether the ailment has a more serious underlying cause.

How's your sleeping been? Do you find you wake up in the night? When was the last time you had a good night's sleep? How's your concentration been? Not too good? And have you been feeling a bit confused? Could that explain why, uncharacteristically, you fell off the ladder while fixing the curtain rail and are now here with a fractured or twisted knee? Have you had any gloomy thoughts lately; fleeting thoughts that life has lost its sparkle, even that it may not be worth living? And, further down the list, have you had any suicidal thoughts or even tried to harm yourself?

With such questions (and more) the astute GP will gradually prise out the real source of the complaint. 'The problem we face with depression,' says Dr Tylee, 'is that it's only the minority of patients who turn up saying they're depressed. The vast majority simply don't know that they are.' It is not surprising, then, that his research into the 'content analysis of consultations' shows that a patient volunteering information about mood swings early on in the consultation was ten times more likely to have clinical depression recognised than someone who referred to such moods obliquely as, say, the twentieth symptom on the check list.

The phenomenon is well attested and referred to as 'masked', 'hidden' or 'unrecognised' depression, a condition which is reckoned to affect 50 per cent of patients passing through the GP's surgery.

The wise and experienced practitioner will be looking for other signs too – not always those that can be put into words. To the trained eye the hunched shoulders, the continual sideways glances, the false smile and so on will convey just as much information as the verbal list of symptoms; to the trained ear the nervous cough, the repeated sigh, even the silence itself are speaking volumes.

But GPs are themselves under tremendous pressure and in a busy surgery such nuances of behaviour can easily, and with the best of intentions, pass by unnoticed. If you can help the doctor to help you then you are already ahead in the process. 'The important thing,' says Dr Tylee, 'is to empower people to know what the symptoms are in advance. Then they can go to the GP and say, "Well, I've got this, this, and this. And I think it might mean I'm depressed. What do you think?"' Or, to put it another way, spotting your own symptoms beforehand will help both the doctor to diagnose the complaint earlier and you to get well sooner. The advice may seem too obvious to state, but it is too important to ignore.

'The first step for the GP,' says Dr Tylee, 'is to get the patient to understand what all those symptoms add up to. And that in itself is therapeutic for most people. So if someone says he's been feeling tired for a year and he can't understand why, and if the GP then explains to him that it's depression, that of itself will often make him feel a bit better.'

Self-diagnosis, of course, is a risky business and 'amateur psychology' is to be recommended with as much reservation as 'home surgery for beginners'. Dr Tylee, more than most, is aware of this. But he and his colleagues are confident enough to have drawn up some basic guidelines. These are contained in the *Defeat Depression* pamphlet published as part of a five-year campaign sponsored by The Royal College of Psychiatrists in association with The Royal College of General Practitioners to 'increase awareness and improve understanding of depression in the community so that those suffering from this common and disabling illness will not be afraid to seek and receive appropriate treatment'.

Symptoms of major depression, the pamphlet states, are indicated by the presence of:

- Depressed mood or loss of interest and pleasure.
- At least four of the following:
  1 Feelings of worthlessness or guilt.
  2 Impaired concentration.
  3 Loss of energy and fatigue.
  4 Thoughts of suicide.
  5 Loss or increase of appetite and weight.
  6 Insomnia (trouble with sleeping) or hypersomnia (too much sleep).
  7 Retardation or agitation.
- At least two weeks duration.
- No evidence of a primary underlying disorder.

From personal experience Dr Tylee knows that depression is an imprecise word. 'You can feel depressed on a Monday morning going in to work. Then half an hour later it's gone and you can forget it. Or you could feel depressed for two or three days – even a week. But it's only when you've got all the other symptoms and it's affecting your functioning that it becomes a problem.'

Clearly one person's problem is another person's challenge and those blessed with a strong constitution (whether emotional or physical) may find their threshold set at a different level than that of their less resilient fellow human beings. But the message is the same for the seven-stone weaklings and the strong, silent types alike. If you are showing at least four of the above symptoms and if the result is that for a period of a fortnight or more your normal functioning is impaired then the alarm bells should start to ring. And you will not be alone if you hear them.

At any one time one person in 20 is reckoned to be affected by depression while one in three of us will experience an attack at least once in our lifetime. According to the Defeat Depression Campaign it goes undetected in up to 70 per cent of cases with the tragic and unnecessary result that it continues to exact its debilitating toll of personal distress and family suffering.

* * *

At its best the family is a wonderfully forgiving and accepting micro-community. Its members, made up of different generations, embody perspectives on life that are contradictory but complementary. It honours its weakest, takes pride in its strongest, and sees worth in its least distinguished and, while striving for the best, is tolerant of individual imperfections. This is an ideal family, of course. However, sometimes, because of its very tolerance, the family is the last to spot the nature of a psychological problem (though among the first to feel its effects).

In Chapter 6 carers (usually husbands and wives) share their experiences of the problems they encounter in looking after those suffering chronic or intermittent depression but for the moment it is helpful to look at another arena of activity, a very public one, where the effects of depressive illness can be felt – the workplace.

Unlike the ideal family here is an environment which is not so unconditionally forgiving and automatically supportive. All the problems resulting from tiredness, lack of motivation, reduced concentration and forgetfulness will be cruelly exposed, subjected to public (and closed door) scrutiny and could have major consequences for an individual's future.

The Department of Health and The Confederation of British Industry have officially recognised depression as a significant phenomenon at work and have estimated that between 15 per cent and 30 per cent of employees will experience some form of mental health problem at some point in their working lives.

Absenteeism and poor performance, which in turn contribute to inefficiency and declining profitability, clearly show themselves in end-of-the-year financial reports. Similarly staff turnover and worrying accident records make a significant impact on company morale which in turn affects output. At its crudest, depression costs money.

In an ideal world of industrial relations, companies would be mirror images of our idealised families where the weak are valued, the strongest are prized and so on. We all know this is not the case. And in times of recession the pressure may be on management to weed out the weakest, and simply get rid of the slowest.

For anyone going through a period of depression such a

realisation merely turns the screw. And, to be fair to management, who are themselves not immune from depressive illness,
they are acutely aware that the demands they make on the shop
floor can ultimately be made of them. The anxiety generated
by this corporate unease drives the sufferer further into his or
her private nightmare with the result that all the attendant
by-products of mood disorder – slowness, carelessness, forgetfulness, poor time-keeping, unexplained absences, disputes and
arguments with colleagues – merely increase.

> 6 I've just taken on a job again after losing one six months ago
> and I've already been warned that my work is not up to stan-
> dard. My concentration is not what it should be and my heart
> is not in it. I worked at my old job in catering for eight years
> and I loved it but after my partner died it became increasingly
> difficult to do. I just couldn't cope with it any more. I tried to
> bury myself in my job to make up for the loss but it simply
> didn't work. 9
>
> *Isabelle, 36, cook*

If, however, an individual can spot in advance a downturn in
mood and the onset of a mental condition which will have physical effects then he or she will be well placed to avoid unnecessary difficulty.

The earlier you can make the decision to see a GP the earlier
you can consult the occupational health department of your
company which in turn might help you to make appropriate
arrangements. If you are not a company worker and if the
notion of contacting an occupational health officer is as realistic
as it would be for a sheet metal worker to request time off to
watch a particularly beautiful sunset there are still measures you
can take.

You alone (though perhaps in consultation with an understanding doctor) can decide how little or how much of your
mental condition you want to make public but letting an
employer know what is going on sooner rather than later is
fairer both to you and to the firm. It also enables the boss to
draw up contingency plans to cover for any absence (which in
most cases will be no more than a few weeks) and to ease your
return to work.

Many people, however, are reluctant to admit to depression at work for fear that it might prejudice their chances of promotion or, worse, that it might actually affect their job security and even result in their being fired. Others worry that it will prejudice their chances of even getting a job in the first place and that, if disclosed on the application form, depression (or any other record of mental illness) will effectively ensure that they are not invited for interview.

The Depression Alliance, a national network of self-help groups, has encountered this particular dilemma on many occasions. Their advice is for sufferers, when applying for a job, not to mention their condition if they are not specifically asked to do so. If they *are* asked to supply details they must, since the deliberate provision of wrong information can be grounds for summary dismissal at a later date. However, if invited merely to tick a box, they might very properly leave it blank but elaborate truthfully at the interview stage.

The fact is that the vast majority of depressives can function perfectly well at work (indeed some become very skilled at disguising their real mood and performing as if they were perfectly all right). And if one uses the oft-repeated example of Winston Churchill it is fair to say that many depressives are able to function at a heightened level of performance and productivity.

Only when there is a more relaxed understanding of what depressive illness involves will public attitudes change. But there are encouraging signs that this process is underway as the fear and the stigma surrounding depression are gradually being chipped away.

3

Professional Help:
A User's Guide

If the first step is recognising depression, the second step is using that insight to do something about it. Or, as Dr Tylee puts it, 'The first step is to get the patient to understand what depression is. And then you need to talk about its natural history. So you have to give them some idea that it is a condition that benefits from pills for symptoms and talk for problems – in a combination approach.'

This is contentious ground. There are those who say depression is 'all in the mind', that drugs will be useless at best and harmful at worst until the underlying cause has been discovered and the root of a (usually childhood) hurt exposed and confronted. On the other hand some clinicians are wary of so-called 'talking therapies' on the grounds that they are a distraction from the 'real' problem which they claim is chemical or electrical – a *physical* malfunction of one of the body's organs.

Whatever the cause of depression, however, there are options available so that you, in collaboration with health professionals, can make an informed choice. Whether this choice takes you ultimately down the clinical path or the counselling path or along a road where both paths converge will depend on the nature and severity of your depression. Take advice at every step along the way. Here are some options:

Friends and Family

These are often the first ports of call in a psychological storm. And rightly so. As the saying goes: that's what friends are for. To be able to confide in friends, to tell them that you are depressed is the most natural thing in the world. But it is as well to be warned that, at times of severe, or even mild clinical depression, they may be of limited value.

For one thing, if they have not been there themselves they will, more than likely, be unable to comprehend the depth of your suffering. They are willing you to get better (they are your friends, after all) but they may be incapable of offering the kind of highly specialised help you need. 'It'll be OK', 'You'll come out of it' and other such soothing phrases are GENUINELY meant but they are unlikely to get you out of the gloom. Entering sympathetically into another person's pain requires a very particular kind of listening skill which does not come naturally to most people. Good listening is often a learnt process which friends and family, with all the best will and intention in the world, may simply not possess.

This is an extract from a conversation, on just this subject, between sufferers of depression.

Joan: You can lose friends when you're depressed.

Neil: It took me a long time to even admit it to my friends.

Nuala: They can't understand.

Nick: No, they can't.

Steve: And a little voice says, 'Don't be too open or they'll think you're a basket case'.

Isabelle: They want to cheer you up but when they see that your mood won't be lifted they can't be bothered.

Nuala: You're more inclined to go to people you don't know. That's why groups work. I phoned up a friend once and she said, 'Oh, what's up, Nuala? Are you fed up again?' Honestly, what can you do? In fact when I feel low I cut myself off from friends – until I feel a bit better. When I'm depressed I have nothing to say to them.

Nick: I often put a mask on with friends and look fairly cheer-ful. Otherwise they say, 'Oh no, Nick is down again'.

This sort of experience is typical. Occasionally, though, an exceptional person will come on the scene – a ministering angel no less but in an everyday disguise. Consider this from Paul Lanham: 'My sister-in-law is wonderful. She used to ring me up two or three times a week to talk about nothing. And it didn't matter. It was just the feeling that there was some life out there. The one thing parents and friends don't understand is how you're feeling. Nobody can get down into that darkness. The only person who's down there is the sufferer. This is the reason why self-help groups are such a godsend.

'A friend (also a sufferer) put her finger on it once. She phoned me at 9.45pm and I said, "How are you?" And she said, "All right". And I thought, "That's not true. Otherwise why are you phoning me at this time of night?" And, of course, it turned out she was having an attack. Eventually she blurted it all out. And at the end she said, "I like talking to you. I feel I can be irrational with you and not be ashamed." That is self-help in a nutshell. When people can be open with each other without any kind of judgmentalism, without having to apologise for how they feel. I'm not saying it's an alternative to orthodox medicine but it's complementary.'

Bear in mind, too, that a friend, even at the best of times, tends to give you the answer he or she thinks you want to hear. In therapeutic terms this is of no use at all. 'Really what friends would be best to do is follow The Samaritans' approach of supportive listening,' says Dr Tylee, 'and to make themselves available day or night and sit there as long as it takes and listen. But very few people can do that.'

In Chapter 5, we will see how The Samaritans have honed down their skills over the years and, in the process, developed techniques that may be of more general use. In the meantime consider one minor success story. It is the story of Nick, a manager in his early 30s, brought down by severe depression. He first spoke to his sister and was fortunate enough to find in her not only a sympathetic listener, but also a woman who had been prone to depression herself and knew what a terrible thing it is to be imprisoned in a darkness which will not admit light. Wisely she did not say she knew how he felt – because she did not. She knew full well how *she* had felt but could not conceivably share his experience. But she could share his pain and, from the depths of her own personal knowledge of the condition, offer genuine and informed sympathy. Moreover, since she was familiar with all that the health professionals had to offer (and aware of their limitations) she could direct Nick first to his GP and then to an organisation specialising in group therapy so that he could feel relaxed enough to talk his feelings through. It was an obvious piece of advice but it came with a loving hand round the shoulder and from a close relative who was yet able to stand back.

Nick's sister proved to be a helpful relative and a loving companion but she knew, also, that there are times when it is best to remove oneself from the familiarity of friends and seek out the comfort of strangers.

The GP

Pressure on the family doctor's time which is, of necessity, limited seems to be increasing. It is not reasonable, therefore, to expect to see immediate results after your first visit. The sympathetic and experienced GP can provide some treatments and can delegate others. For instance, Dr Tylee's approach is to consider medication for the symptoms and talk for the problem, a twin-track approach that has the backing of The Royal College of Psychiatrists and The Royal College of General Practitioners. This means that a course of treatment will be designed to suit the individual needs of one patient and may be totally unsuitable for another.

According to Dr Tylee, 'If they have depression bad enough to need pills, then pills will actually help. But I have to tell them that the tablets will take two or three weeks to start working and that once they have begun a course of tablets they need to stay on that dose for four to six weeks afterwards because, if they don't, there's a 50-50 chance the symptoms will come back again. And so you have to give out all these key messages to get the patient's agreement and compliance to take medication.'

But it is important to stress, he says, that this is only part of the whole picture. 'The pills will only really help the symptoms.' An attendant underlying problem may have to be tackled through other means. So in practice, a particular medication may improve, say, a patient's sleep pattern but it may not address the cause of his or her fitful sleep. However, by getting more satisfactory rest that same patient will be helped to function better and this may, in turn, help them to benefit more from the 'talking treatments' if these are thought appropriate.

Dr Tylee also talks to his patients. And at the same time that he is prescribing a course of tablets for symptoms he is asking himself and his patient whether any of the underlying problems might be addressed as well. As he puts it, 'I'd be thinking, "does this person have problems which are soluble? Are there things he can fruitfully talk over with his wife or his employer to help get him out of this difficulty?" You might break down his problems bit by bit and encourage him to do something constructive about them. You might suggest he makes an appointment with the bank manager to defer a mortgage repayment or something. Then if patients have problems which are insoluble you help them with coping strategies. This is harder but it is basically supportive. A bereavement is an obvious example of the kind of thing which cannot be 'put right'. To a lesser though equally intractable degree, there may be a problem of housing. If someone cannot get rehoused from the 18th floor of a tower block then they will have to be encouraged to cope until such time as the situation changes.'

Other life events might be redundancy, or divorce – any number of things which cannot be changed but merely endured. In these circumstances the advice is not simply 'to grin and bear it' but to explore imaginatively what adjustments can be made to make these new, unexpected, and, frankly, unpleasant experiences tolerable.

Dr Tylee might recommend they join a self-help group like the Depression Alliance, for example, in order for them to exchange stories with fellow sufferers. 'They'll get support from this,' he says, 'if they go along on a weekly basis. Or they might find someone they can phone up in between, or perhaps there's a Samaritan who they can link up with from time to time. As long as they have some contact when the times are bad they can then ventilate their feelings.'

On occasions, a longer and more difficult process of acceptance might be called for. In such circumstances a counsellor's sensitivity will be tested to the limit. But in skilled and caring hands a bruised individual need not be broken. The motto here is deceptively and sometimes painfully simple. It is spoken softly, with infinite kindness, and in complete humility: Accept what you cannot change. Change what you can.

The psychologist

There are a number of specialisms within the discipline of psychology and you can be advised by a GP as to which branch may be suitable for you – if at all. In some cases you can be referred and have treatment on the NHS but frequently such services are only available in the private sector.

In a practice specifically geared to the treatment of depression (these are comparatively rare) there will be a small team of individuals trained in psychology and working closely with a GP. There might, for example, be a counselling psychologist who deals with patients passed on by the doctor and who engages in 'talking therapies'. The benefit of such a person is that he or she can give far more time to helping patients through their difficulties than a GP can in the surgery time available.

In addition there might be a clinical psychologist on hand who takes on the more specialised forms of therapy, and under his or her supervision organises group therapy. These are highly focused sessions and not simply random conversations (helpful as these can sometimes be). A particularly useful kind of therapy in some cases is cognitive therapy.

Cognitive therapy

This is a form of treatment which aims, through talking, to 'correct' an imbalance in a person's perceptions. An individual who is depressed will typically have a low sense of his or her own worth. And this low self-esteem will tend to make people see things in a uniformly negative light. They will see someone in the street, for example, and wave excitedly. When the person does not respond (for whatever reason) they will assume the fault is automatically theirs; that they have done something to upset them, that they shouldn't have waved so much because it has embarrassed them and frightened them off, or that they are worthless and insignificant specimens whom no one would want to acknowledge anyway. Through cognitive therapy these assumptions would be challenged. Perhaps the person hadn't heard them, perhaps he or she was shortsighted and hadn't seen them, or perhaps they were just preoccupied and dashing for a bus.

Patients are encouraged to test out their usually negative perceptions against other more positive possibilities. One way of doing this is to keep a diary of all the depressive thoughts and feelings they might have had in a week and then to talk through these entries with the therapist. 'I'm always messing things up, I never see anything through,' a patient might say. 'Well, let's look at the week's events,' comes the reply. 'What about the appointment you were going to make with the dentist? Did you make it?'

'Yes.'

'And the cake you were going to bake for your goddaughter? Did you make it?'

'Yes.'

'Were you pleased with it?'

'Yes.'

'What about the tickets you were going to book for that show?'

'Well, I didn't get round to it. I sort of got cold feet' . . . . and so on.

At the end of a session the therapist can say, 'Well, OK, you didn't get round to four things you were hoping to do. But these three you did perfectly well. You can't say you NEVER see anything through, can you? You're not ALWAYS messing things up, are you?'

The same pattern of questions and answers might also be used to confront feelings of worthlessness in relationships; to challenge ingrained and erroneous assumptions that 'nobody likes me, everybody ignores me' and so on. In conversations like these a therapist can challenge automatic thinking and, over a period of time, encourage the patient to get a balanced perspective on his or her life. According to Dr Tylee, studies have shown that this form of therapy, when handled responsibly by a trained practitioner, can be quite successful in achieving a turn-around in automatic thinking and having a lasting and beneficial effect.

A word of warning. This is a shorthand account of ONE ASPECT of what the therapy might involve. Inevitably it is over-simplified. Individuals considering such therapy should first seek advice as to whether it might be appropriate, and then consult only someone who is qualified and accredited with a recognised professional body.

Inevitably the sessions will be lengthy and protracted. And while GPs might borrow from such techniques they would be unable, in the consultation time available, to give such treatment themselves. This they might delegate to a psychologist who might not expect to see results until, say, the patient had attended 18 weekly one-hour sessions.

For Dr Tylee the importance of the psychologist is in complementing the treatment he is also dispensing. The psychologist might help in problem solving, in suggesting coping strategies (visiting the bank manager to explain why an overdraft can't yet be cleared etc), and in teaching an individual how to manage stress which, in turn, may be adding to the depression.

The psychotherapist

Jonathan, now in his late 30s, has been depressed for as long as he can remember. 'The depression was there when I was a child but I wouldn't have known what to call it then. It was just a feeling of rejection I suppose. I could never be what was expected of me. It all goes back to when I was four and my father gave me an IQ test. After I got a high score I was never allowed to be a child again. I was always supposed to behave according to my intellectual age as opposed to my physical age. So I lost out on childhood.'

The experience of carrying round depression for what seems like a lifetime is common. Peter, a journalist in his early 40s, says typically, 'I feel I've been depressed for over 30 years.' The depression then becomes the backdrop against which every aspect of one's life is lived. 'The great mass of men,' said the American poet and essayist Henry Thoreau, 'lead lives of quiet desperation.' And while this chronic low-level despair will often not prevent individuals from leading what are outwardly highly successful lives, it will taint the emotional response they make to the world – limiting them and keeping them prisoners, albeit in a golden cage, of unfulfilled promise. Then an event happens which triggers a dramatic reaction. It may be the death of a friend, the loss of a job, or the birth of a child which triggers the change but that change, when it comes, can threaten all that once seemed so stable.

So it was with Peter. He had noticed that his moods, not helped by the recent death of his mother, had been slowly getting worse. He was at a loss to understand why he should suddenly become tearful while taking the Tube into work, or why he was forgetting the simplest of things, often repeating what he had just said or stopping mid-sentence to let his thoughts trail off into nothingness. He was refusing to notice, despite the fact that his wife was often bringing it to his attention, that he was drinking more and more. Indeed once he drew up a list of the alcohol 'units' he had consumed in one week and while he was alarmed that the total amounted to four times what was recommended he did little or nothing to cut down his intake.

One evening after a drunken dinner out with his work colleagues he made an uncharacteristic pass at a secretary and embarked on a brief but disastrous affair. The marriage came under enormous strain and after furious rows Peter and his wife agreed to a trial separation. Friends suggested that the couple should see the marriage guidance organisation, Relate, and a sympathetic counsellor suggested in turn that Peter might benefit from an appointment with a psychotherapist.

Reluctant to go along in the first place Peter finally relented and began a course of counselling which was to last nearly two years. During regular weekly sessions he was encouraged to explore the root of his unease by talking. He began to realise that he had never opened himself up in this way before. As an only child he had led a largely self-contained life with few if any upsets. With increasing clarity, however, he saw that while his parents had striven hard to give him the material things in life they had isolated him emotionally, often leaving him on his own in the house, and rarely, if ever, playing with him.

The more Peter was allowed to talk openly the more he realised the depth of the emotional deprivation he had been carrying around for so long. And once he accepted it all he was able to move forward. He allowed himself to grieve over the death of his mother – an event which, unbeknown to him, had been responsible for propelling him into the briefly comforting (though ultimately destructive) solace of drink and an adulterous affair.

Armed with the knowledge of what it was that was eating at him he was able to change his behaviour through an effort of will and to spot signs of a downturn in mood and take evasive action. His drinking stabilised, he began to take regular exercise, to make time for his wife and children and the marriage was rescued from the brink of collapse. His background depression was also brought under control.

At its best and most successful this is the kind of result a trained psychotherapist can bring about. The client is simply encouraged to talk – to talk with the kind of frankness that might be impossible with either a friend or a GP. And because the psychotherapist is able to explore areas of great intimacy within a framework of professional distance a unique and trusting relationship can develop within which the most painful aspects of personal experience can be given an airing.

The process is not immediate and conversations in the therapist's room may get emotionally uncomfortable at times. There may be long silences or moments of great emotion when a person's past hurts come agonisingly to the surface. Things may have to get worse before they get better as childhood pain is relived long after the client thought it had been buried.

As the Bible says of good and corrupt trees, 'By their fruits you shall know them'. The same principle applies with psychotherapy. If the process is suitable for you and if there is a discernible beneficial effect then you will know that the therapy has been worth while. In the hands of a skilled and compassionate counsellor a person can be encouraged to confront his or her past and to heal some of the hurts that have cast a shadow over the adult years.

It is advisable to discuss your intentions first with a GP who may be in a position to recommend someone to you. Increasingly general practices incorporate a counselling element in their work and will sometimes have a trained counsellor or psychologist on the premises. It is also advisable to keep your partner informed of what you intend to do. The discovery, half-way through a session, that you have been undergoing 'secret' treatment and may be revealing the most intimate details of your (and somebody else's) life can induce a feeling similar to betrayal – as if one partner were cutting the other out of his or her life entirely.

This does not mean, however, that all aspects of the therapy will have to be discussed over dinner at home. You are allowed your confidences, after all. Indeed, it is likely that if a partner knows from the outset that your therapy, though confidential, is not a matter for secrecy then he or she will not feel threatened by your treatment.

The years of loneliness or emotional cruelty, the instances of physical or mental abuse as a vulnerable child, and the infancy scarred by loss will not be wiped away with a therapist's magic wand but they can be confronted and eventually healed. Your personal demons may never ultimately be chased away but they can, with help, be tamed.

If you are ever in London pay a visit to the National Gallery in Trafalgar Square and spend a few moments in front of Uccello's painting of St George and the Dragon. It is a curiously compelling picture which, to my mind, offers a useful insight into the process of psychotherapy. To the left is the damsel in distress, to the right is St George, and between them is the ferocious monster threatening to wreak havoc in both their lives. St George charges in manfully, his lance at the ready, prepared to kill the beast and to remove it from their lives.

The damsel's reaction is interesting. For a start she is not in distress at all. On the contrary she is perfectly serene. She has chosen a different method of confronting her personal dragon. Unlike St George perhaps she realises that the causes of her deepest fears cannot be erased or annihilated with a simple thrust of the lance. Instead they have to be accommodated. And to do this she elects not to kill the dragon but to tame it. And look closely again. She has succeeded and reached contentment. For the dragon is on a lead and, although St George is too occupied to notice, the other end of the lead is in the damsel's steady hand.

The psychiatrist

A GP will refer to a psychiatrist a patient suffering only the most serious mental disorder – of which depression might be only one (albeit acute) component part. It is reckoned that 5 per cent of patients passing through the doctor's surgery with such disorders will be referred to a psychiatrist and among these will be those suffering from depression which is not responding to treatment.

A psychiatrist is a qualified doctor; a trained physician, licensed to prescribe drugs, and someone who has chosen to specialise in a particular branch of medicine devoted to the treatment of mental and emotional disorders.

One of the primary reasons, according to Dr Tylee, for sending a patient to a psychiatrist is if the patient has suicidal intent. 'I would be worried,' he says, 'that left on their own they would kill themselves. So that would be my overriding concern. Another worry I would have is if they lived alone and might come to grief by neglect. The next reason for referring is if I am treating someone and the treatment is simply not working. And they may be getting worse not better. Moreover a psychiatrist would often take over from me if the patient has depression complicated by some other condition, say, drug abuse, alcoholism, anorexia, or a phobia of some kind. In rarer cases I might refer because I am being pressurised to do so by the family. Perhaps they can't cope with a behavioural difficulty or whatever and they insist on a referral more for their peace of mind than for mine or the patient's.'

What characterises referral is severity. In the instance just described the family of the sufferer clearly judged his or her behaviour to be so alarming and so impervious to the current treatment that another line of attack was needed. Inevitably, then, the psychiatrist will be confronted with complex conditions.

Should you find yourself being referred for such treatment because of severe depressions there are a couple of points to bear in mind. The first is that you are not an oddity. You are ill. And illnesses can be cured. The second is that there is no reason to be nervous. If you are feeling nervous you might be invited to bring a relative or a friend to the first consultation (usually an hour) when a series of quite painless questions about your past medical history and your present psychological condition will be asked.

Remember, too, that the psychiatrist is not an oddity either. He or she is a doctor – a special kind of doctor but still a doctor whose aim is to get you well again. 'One of the things our training makes us rather good at is diagnosis,' says consultant psychiatrist, Sally Pidd. 'We are able to look at a condition from a number of different perspectives.' In practice this means that though *psychologists* would look at a depressed person and be able to assess the role of childhood, of background, of environment and of behaviour they would not be able to apply a medical model to the condition itself. The *psychiatrist* would. 'What we could do is rule out certain medical causes of depression; an underactive thyroid gland, for example, which can make people sluggish, or a brain tumour which would have a definite impact on behaviour and mood. If someone were complaining of tiredness, for example, I could check for causes other than possible depression. I might do a physical examination to rule out anaemia; I would check blood pressure, pulse rate and so on.'

What the psychiatrist is doing is bringing into play an elaborate though highly targeted screening procedure – ruling out certain possible causes of depression and bringing other perhaps overlooked possibilities into the frame. Undiagnosed alcoholism might, for example, be a contributory factor or, in some cases, long-term and sustained use of cannabis.

But Dr Pidd admits there can sometimes be disadvantages in the purely medical approach. 'I suppose the drawback is that it's always easier to give someone a pill than to practise long-term psychotherapy, because pills are quick to dispense and psychotherapy is not.' Not, of course, that psychiatrists merely dole out tablets. The trend nowadays is for doctors to use a multidisciplinary approach in the care of depression and Dr Pidd, for example, familiar with the techniques of psychotherapy, borrows from them when she thinks it appropriate.

In addition to looking at the physical constitution of an individual, she asks more complex psychological questions about irrational guilt, feelings of worthlessness, thoughts of suicide and the like – all by way of painting an overall picture of the mental condition under scrutiny. 'I would want to know about previous psychiatric history, and, in particular, whether there is any mental illness in the family. Does a person have a genetic predisposition to depressive illness, for example? Why is this person coming for help now? Have there been instances of deliberate self-harm? Has there been a suicide attempt?

'I would also ask whether they had had episodes of feeling the very opposite of depressed, moments when they become overactive, elated, extravagant . . . a bit over the top.' A 'Yes' to this last question might indicate manic depression which responds quite well to medication. Certain drugs are useful in controlling the mood swings associated with this condition and can be used in turn to stabilise the depression.

At this point you may be wondering whether such medication can do you damage and whether it can actually take away an aspect of your personality. Some people may, for example, have naturally ebullient tendencies which are heightened when the mood is on the up. Might stabilising the depression also involve ironing out those natural highs and therefore interfering with an individual's personality – shades of *One Flew Over The Cuckoo's Nest*? It is a philosophical question which all psychiatrists have considered. This is how Dr Pidd views it – as always, from the patient's point of view. 'Most people who are depressed don't like being depressed. And they see nothing beneficial about *being* depressed. So having the depression treated can be only to the good.' In other words, should you find yourself referred to a psychiatrist it is, as with any other doctor, your well-being which will be paramount.

However, at the mention of 'electric shock treatment' (an erroneous phrase conjuring up quite the wrong impression) many people feel that their well-being is being sacrificed on an altar of near barbarous clinical intervention. Although much debate surrounds the use of ECT (electroconvulsive therapy) its benefits for some patients are undeniable.

The first electroconvulsive treatment was administered in 1938 and was experimental in nature. The following year it began to be clinically assessed in Britain but, even before the results were properly known, it was being used quite widely and indiscriminately. With the application of anaesthetics and muscle relaxants the procedure is now, medically speaking, very safe – with a risk factor comparable to that found in other surgical operations requiring a general anaesthetic. However, given the nature of the process, ECT still continues to be thought of with a mixture of fear and suspicion. Delivering an electric shock to the brain in order deliberately to induce an epileptic seizure seems a strange expression of medical care.

Of its early history Dr Pidd has this to say: 'It was the first treatment that was commonly used in the big "asylums" and was pretty crude at the outset. The observation was made that people with schizophrenia did not seem to have epilepsy very often.' From this starting point doctors then wondered whether, by somehow reversing the process and inducing a fit in the patient, the schizophrenia would get better. By and large it did not. But before those conclusions emerged doctors had begun to put a whole range of other patients, including depressives, on ECT and something that they had not predicted began to happen. The depressed patients appeared to make a marked improvement.

Much research, as well as fierce controversy, surrounds the technique and there seems to be no conclusive explanation as to why passing an electric current through a patient's brain might have beneficial consequences (when common sense suggests that the reverse should apply). 'You could read a whole tome on it,' says Dr Pidd, 'but there isn't a straightforward answer. There was quite a lot of research done in the 80s to see whether it was the placebo effect at work. Because, as you can imagine, it is a bit of a palaver. You have to give someone an anaesthetic, so you have to starve them from midnight. Then in the morning you go off to the treatment room where they have a muscle relaxant and an injection to put them to sleep. They come round five minutes later feeling a bit groggy and they have a cup of tea and a lot of fuss is made of them.' In such circumstances the patient may simply *feel* that he is feeling better. And as a result he does indeed feel better. 'But,' says Dr Pidd, 'controlled trials of ECT were done in the 80s which I think did prove that there was something about the electric current which did get people better.'

ECT is usually offered to patients who have failed to respond to a course of anti-depressants although it is sometimes offered as a first option to those who are unwilling to follow a course of drug treatment (for fear, perhaps, of side-effects), or to those who have responded well to ECT in the past. It is also considered in extreme circumstances as a means of offering swift treatment to someone in severe distress.

All case histories are different, of course, and it would be foolish to assume that a technique which has proved successful for one person will transfer automatically to another. However, one instance Sally Pidd cites gives some insight into how a combination of treatments can be used to beneficial effect. Some of the detail that follows has been changed in the interests of confidentiality.

One man, let us call him Alan, was admitted to a northern hospital with severe depression. The distinguishing factor in his case was that each depressive bout was accompanied by the obsessive conviction that he was being followed. All this stemmed back to an essentially trivial incident some 25 years earlier when he had borrowed some tools from a university department and failed to return them.

When Alan is well there are no shadowy figures in pursuit of him. When he is depressed they are everywhere; in the red car over there, skulking by the bus stop across the road, watching him from the library bookshelves – and all because of this misdemeanour 25 years ago.

He seeks reassurance all the time and, while he is not excited, he is in a permanent state of total anxiety. No amount of reassurance can calm him. So far only a combination of ECT and medication has managed to bring his condition under control. And if, when his moods have returned to normal, Sally Pidd asks where his mysterious pursuers are, he replies, 'Oh, now you come to mention it, I haven't seen them lately.'

If a talking therapy is possible in Alan's case it has not, despite extensive efforts, been found yet. One is left with the question: is it better to leave him (and his wife) in some distress by withholding the invasive therapy?

* * *

'One of the strengths of a discipline like psychiatry,' says Dr Pidd, 'is that we're quite good at categorising things. I know you could also call it a weakness but I think it's quite a strength to be able to say that you have heard a person's story before and you know quite quickly which box to put it into.' There are nuances within each individual case, of course, but the patient benefits by having a broadly standard type of treatment waiting in the wings. 'We have a diagnostic framework which enables us to say that this sort of treatment will help that sort of patient. Without this framework everything is a one-off. You are inventing the wheel all the time.'

But the framework is only a framework, an essentially theoretical model which is used to interpret the real world. And Dr Pidd knows from experience that the real world is never as neat and tidy as the framework. To take bereavement, for example, which is one of the major life experiences likely to promote a major downturn in mental well-being. 'If you have talked to lots of people who have been bereaved,' she says, 'you will see how varied the response is. Ordinary people without a history of mental illness will fall apart when someone close to them dies. Then eventually they get things back together again. There are other people who have a stiff upper lip for a few months until a trigger sets off a major reversal. Then there are others who are just sad, and who remain sad with an abiding sense of loss. Then there are some people who just blot out the experience completely and go into a state of denial. Others get very angry and threaten to sue everybody in sight. Some start campaigns or whatever. So there are all these different bereavement responses.'

How to interpret these responses is the dilemma facing all the professionals. And how to sift out perfectly normal and under-standable sadness from chronic, destructive depression is the first of a complex series of decisions that they have to make.

At the extreme end of the spectrum the psychiatrist can be confronted with a pathological response. Dr Pidd explains, 'What we are talking about is something out of the range of ordinary reaction.' So, a week after bereavement a newly widowed man turns over one morning in bed expecting his wife to be beside him. She is not. In agony he moves closer to the spot where she once lay and holds the pillow to himself kissing it desperately as he weeps inconsolably. Such a reaction is quite normal. 'But,' says Dr Pidd, 'if this is still happening two years on and the man is equally distraught, I would have to conclude that this is an abnormal bereavement reaction.'

Treatment at this point is possible but it is clearly much better to recognise the signs of depression at an earlier stage before it has taken such a hold on the individual in question. Faced with an abnormal bereavement the psychiatrist might accompany the patient through a process of grieving – first, to get the person simply to acknowledge that a partner *has* died, then to talk about all aspects of that partner's life and personality. 'It may be like going through a series of exercises,' says Dr Pidd who her-self works closely with a colleague specialising in bereavement counselling. 'You might ask someone to write a letter to their dead husband or wife, for example. People are often left with regrets about what they did or didn't say to someone and they wish they had been able to round things off.' Writing a letter, holding an imaginary conversation, or perhaps visiting the grave and actually saying goodbye are all possible ways dealing with the unavoidable sadness of the event before it has a chance to change into something more intractable.

Dr Pidd knows, however, that things can go either way. Take the example of a patient who lost his wife unexpectedly. 'He sees absolutely no point in living. In his depression he has said that if his wife is not here he doesn't want to be here either. He's just slowly starving himself to death. He's lost five or six stone so far and there's not much we can do about it.'

Compare this reaction with one she encountered in a local hospice. Although there can be (and frequently is) much sadness in an institution specialising in the care of the dying there need not automatically be depression. Where it does occur it can be treated. The man in question had cancer which had been diagnosed as terminal. At the most he had a few months to live. His immediate reaction was to go into decline. He became withdrawn, refused to eat, and stopped talking to people around him. He had set himself against life and had decided he was simply going to die. The staff knew that such a reaction was out of character and that he was undergoing a bout of depression which, in addition to his cancer, was having a very distressing effect on his wife. He had even refused to speak to her and had apparently decided to retreat completely into himself.

Anti-depressants had failed to work so, in consultation with Dr Pidd, the staff decided on a course of ECT – even though the patient had an extremely short time to live. As a result of four treatment sessions the staff noticed a distinct upturn in his mood. He started to talk again, to sit up in bed and to take an interest in things around him. Crucially, though, he and his wife used the last six weeks of his life to talk. Simply to talk. And it is not hard to imagine that such emotional intimacy was enormously healing. 'We hadn't cured him,' says Dr Pidd, 'but we had achieved a qualitative difference in his life. There was an enormous change in his outlook. From having his face set firmly against the wall he was transformed into a person who was able to recognise that, even with a terminal illness, there was something that could be done to make life better.'

Because the psychiatrist is able to view depression in a medical framework – and to dispense medical treatment in the form of drugs or ECT accordingly – he or she is able to use a variety of means to tackle the underlying problem. 'We often see people who have got into a downward spiral because their life has got into a mess in one way or another,' says Dr Pidd. 'I was treating a man who was depressed, off work, and simply not coping with life. He had had marital problems for three years and now things were on the edge of collapse – or possibly over the edge.'

She prescribed anti-depressants as a result of which his mood lifted a little. What was important in the next stage was that he could use this improvement in mood, small though it was, to start talking to his wife about their difficulties. He could also get back to work which in turn contributed to a greater sense of well-being. 'Once he had got the spiral going round in the right way he had enough energy to put into sorting out his problems for himself.'

What Dr Pidd and others have found is that the correct drug can create a window of opportunity for the sufferer, enabling him or her to make some small improvement in life. The result is that the patient can use this improved state to make further improvements and the process becomes a cumulative one. Many anti-depressants contain a sedative, for example, which will give a person better rest. If that person can merely get a good night's sleep once in a while the likelihood is that he or she can tap into renewed sources of energy to make practical changes in life.

The prognosis is all very well for some. But what of others whose depression is brought on by a life event which cannot be changed? No amount of medication, for example, will provide a job for someone who has been made redundant in mid-life. This is a classic problem for those involved in the treatment of depression. But even this is capable of resolution.

Take another, not untypical case history. A woman in her 30s is bogged down in a stagnant life with an unsupportive husband who, while unemployed, does nothing around the house to help and who leaves every aspect of caring for their three small children to her. Deciding on a course of self-improvement to make life more tolerable she enrols at a college and studies for a degree. Things go well and she shows real promise until she discovers that the husband has been gambling away the domestic finances and they are £2,000 in mortgage arrears. She must now put the studying on hold while she goes out to work to earn money.

The downward spiral is beginning to turn. When she comes back home in the evenings she has to go out again to work in a bar and, as a result, is constantly tired. She is short tempered with the children whose behaviour consequently gets worse – only increasing her stress. She develops psychosomatic back pain which keeps her off work and prevents her from bailing out the family finances.

This is a strong and capable woman being squeezed from all sides. And, as a result of outside circumstances largely unrelated to her, this strong and capable woman is having difficulty coping. She is screaming at the kids, driven to fury by her husband's fecklessness, and worried that the house will be repossessed. On top of this she has to hobble back to work in pain to put in over 40 hours a week AND consider settling down to study to produce the six essays that are overdue and without which her course will be terminated.

It is hardly surprising that her depression is acute and that it is preventing her from functioning normally. An anti-depressant is prescribed and gradually her mood begins to lift, taking her to a level where it is possible once again at least to think straight and plan a strategy.

One psychiatrist who dealt with a similar case described the process of treatment like this: 'Although it's not what a psychiatrist is paid or trained to do, we were able to sit down together, look at a seemingly impossible scenario, and devise a list of priorities. It's a case of looking creatively at a mess and deciding what, in very trying circumstances, can be done in the short and medium term to allow for long-term recovery.'

What this meant in practice was that the woman could use the small improvement in her mood to do one positive thing at a time. First she told the bank manager that there was a problem but that the problem was in the process of being dealt with. Then, with her mind more at ease, she asked for a delay in the essay deadline. Another minor relief ensued during which she now had the strength to talk to her husband firmly but constructively. Bit by bit she regained control over her life which in turn eased her depression.

4
Ways Out

The majority of depressed people do nothing terribly dramatic with their lives (though, as we shall see in the next chapter, some tragically do). Most of them simply go on – at great personal cost to themselves – with, what is for them, the dreary business of living. There are no medals for such people, nor any citations for courage in the face of the enemy (and depression *is* the enemy, unpredictable and elusive, lying patiently in wait, armed with a well-prepared strategy for ambush and capture). Their monumental efforts at mere survival deserve (but rarely get) recognition, admiration and even respect.

What the world sees is Alan or Sarah, long-faced as usual, sighing in the canteen, refusing all entreaties to brighten up or to come out for a drink in the evening after work. This is the side they present to their colleagues who, in turn, see only a Mr or a Ms Misery in their midst habitually defeated by life. But were they to know of the fight that many have put up they would almost certainly revise their opinions. For many, even getting dressed and making their way to work in the first place is an achievement in itself.

Paul Lanham, whose promising career as an Anglican priest was cut short by mental illness, puts it this way: 'The snag is that depression is very debilitating and your first feeling every morning as soon as you wake is of being kicked in the stomach. There is just the terror at the thought of a new day.'

Or this from Nick:

> ❛I'd wake up and the depression would be on me straight away. I couldn't do the simplest thing. If the telephone rang I couldn't pick it up. The absolute depression and terror just blanked out my head. It was as if part of my brain had just closed down.❜

Merely keeping that terror in check requires immense reserves of strength and will-power. Indeed the mental gymnastics a depressed person will often be forced to perform to keep body and soul together are beyond most people's comprehension. Paul's strategy was to think of his family, and this gave him a tenuous thread of self-esteem to cling on to. 'Self-esteem is vital when you're depressed,' he says. 'You have to believe that you are a valid member of society and that you have something to offer to the world.'

The outside world could have seen that, when well, Paul had an enormous amount to give to his parishioners. He was hard working and understanding, efficient and compassionate – in short, good at his job. But when he was ill, his sense of self-worth dwindled to a trickle. 'With the family,' he says, 'I reduced myself to the level of an insurance policy. And in some ways this is what kept me going. As long as I was alive there was a roof over their heads. Thanks to me, although it might have been hell on earth for them inside the house, at least they had somewhere to live. It sounds crazy to say it but I reasoned that financially I was worth more to them alive than dead. So I kept going. That's how things are down there in the depression.'

His plight was not helped by his upbringing. 'I come from a stiff-upper-lip background where talking or even thinking about mental illness is taboo. You never show emotion under those circumstances. I was brought up in the vicarage and sent to public school at an early age. Talking about my feelings was something I simply didn't do. You've got your background against you.'

Steve, a computer programmer in his mid-thirties, comes from a completely different background but registers the same reaction to the daily challenge of what for others is normal life. 'You make your lists of things to do,' he says, 'but what you have to force yourself to do are the trivial things. Change your socks. Get up. It's as desperate as that. And if you manage to do these little jobs, it's a great triumph at the time.'

And having made the heroic effort merely to change his socks he then has to think about putting in a day's work at the office. It is as if, having climbed Everest without oxygen before breakfast, the depressive is then told he really ought to ski down it before lunch. Oh, and when he's done that, there's something else planned for the afternoon and evening. For the depressed person ordinary life presents a constant series of major challenges which others merely take in their stride.

Night-time brings no let-up. Says Steve, 'There's this nasty purgatorial state when you're neither awake nor asleep thinking, "Oh, God. Oh, God." I live near Big Ben and one night I heard it strike once. And I thought to myself that I couldn't be bothered to get out of bed to look at my watch and check the time. So I had to lie there for 45 minutes before I knew what it was quarter past. Somebody couldn't believe I was in such a state and said I must have pinched the story from a Tony Hancock routine. I hadn't, of course. I was not awake and not asleep, I was just sort of flaked out. It was very unpleasant and left me feeling as if I was floating in a kind of fully conscious paralysis.'

One of the worst things about depression is its capacity to swallow up all other feelings, sensations, experiences and emotions into itself. At its worst it is the depression alone which exists. All other independent life has ceased to operate. A sufferer becomes almost literally defined by the suffering. 'If you're not depressed,' says Steve, 'a nice sticky cake or ten quid on the scratchcards can cheer you up. When you're depressed none of those activities are possible. You think of life as a whole as totally pointless. You can stare at the ceiling for months.'

And many do. So one feels like orchestrating a round of applause for those who resist the gravitational pull of early morning depression and make the supreme effort merely to get up and to face the day at all. Confronted with such unremitting effort, some people, hardly surprisingly, take to 'self-medication' to blot it out. This is as dangerous a course of action as it is outwardly seductive.

To give yourself up to the initially comforting but transitory and ultimately destructive lure of alcohol and drug abuse is to make an easy but colossal mistake. Statistics show that many make it all the time. After the death of her husband and after intermittent bouts of depression brought on, in part at least, by her constant feelings of being an outsider in English society

Lisa, who had been born in Austria and who settled in England shortly after the Second World War, felt she could not bear the misery of it all.

She found that taking a drink in the afternoon was a means of dulling the pain. However, she soon realised that the 'medication' she had chosen to administer was subject to the law of diminishing returns. While one drink took the edge off the depression at first, soon she needed two drinks to achieve the same effect. The more she drank the more she needed to drink and so the downward spiral began. What started as a means of getting her out of the depression ended by compounding it – thus rendering her condition harder to treat.

When complicated by alcohol or drug addiction, depression becomes an increasingly acute threat to long-term mental and physical well-being. It can also have a disastrous effect on those people closest to a sufferer, that is to say, on the very people who might be able to help most.

Ian began to use drink as a sedative, as something that would, quite simply, put him out for the count. Having endured night upon night of sleeplessness he took to drinking more and more. In a relationship at the time, he found himself becoming gradually out of step with his girlfriend. 'I couldn't sleep so I'd drink,' he says. 'That meant she would go to bed while I stayed up. The next day I'd be tired as soon as I woke up and the tiredness would last all day. When I came home in the evening I got into the habit of lying down for a while until the "while" got longer and longer.' When he did wake up the tiredness had gone but by now his girlfriend was thinking about going to bed herself. Unable to sleep Ian would start to drink alone and so the cycle repeated itself.

The fact is that alcohol is a *depressant* not a stimulant. And while it seems to be giving our mood a lift it is achieving that effect by *depressing* our inhibitions. Long-term use of alcohol will merely make your depression worse, contribute to a greater sense of anxiety in the morning and, if you are taking anti-depressants at the time, reduce the effectiveness of the medication.

If you are concerned about possible alcohol abuse you should ask yourself the following questions:

- Do you find it difficult to stop drinking once you have started?
- Do you drink alone or in secret?
- Do you need a drink to get you through the day/evening?
- Are your drinking habits overshadowing your other interests?
- Have you ever forgotten what happened during a drinking bout?
- Do you need a drink to boost your self-confidence?

If you find yourself answering 'Yes' to one or more of these questions you may have a problem with alcohol which it is wise to admit to yourself or your GP. If unchecked it is likely to get worse and this, in turn, can only increase depression.

For alcohol also read drugs. Any substance on which you find yourself relying which has not been prescribed by a doctor should be viewed with grave suspicion. And this leaves out of the equation any subconscious anxiety caused by taking illegal drugs, a factor that is likely to deepen your depression still further.

Depression in adolescents and children may manifest itself in two distinct ways. The first will be similar to adult depression with the young person showing signs of increasing lethargy, staying in bed late, lacking concentration, losing weight, and becoming remote and uncommunicative. The second could take the form of behavioural problems such as truancy, petulant or disobedient moods, and substance abuse.

The temporary high that children may get from glue-sniffing will hold out the same deceptive attraction as alcohol does for an adult. It is often a means of blotting out unpleasant or hurtful feelings and anaesthetising themselves against the world. In Chapter 7 we will look at how good parenting skills can help strengthen a child against depression in later life but for now it is worth pointing out that depression in the young can be caused by a variety of things – from being bullied or taunted at school to being sexually abused or emotionally maltreated.

Depression may also result from unresolved grief at the death of a grandparent, say, or even at the death of a pet. Rejection by a girl- or boyfriend is not to be minimised, either. Crushes and longings during the adolescent years are at their most intense and idealistic; disappointment, unrequited love and sexual jealousy are correspondingly hard to bear.

In normal circumstances these will be borne with greater or lesser degrees of fortitude and accepted as part of the manageable series of trials and tribulations that attend the untidy business of growing up. If such rejections occur in the context of chronic emotional neglect, however, then they may trigger a potentially more serious depressive condition.

Since children will lack the emotional vocabulary to express their feelings and since adolescents may be reluctant anyway to communicate their feelings to parents and teachers, the diagnosis of depression is difficult. Bear in mind that depressive moods can be turned inwards or outwards. If internalised they are likely to lead to tiredness, remoteness and a lack of interest in things that once gave them pleasure, whereas, if externalised, they can produce various kinds of disruptive or anti-social behaviour and, in extreme cases, violence.

What both states are likely to have in common is a growing sense of alienation from the world around. If you are fortunate enough to have kept good lines of communication open with your teenage children (and this means developing them very early on, and maintaining them through childhood) then a straightforward heart to heart may be beneficial. In the case of more intractable disorders which are having a negative or destructive effect on a young person's development it may be necessary, via the GP, to consider referral to a family psychologist or even a child psychiatrist.

It is not uncommon for troubled adolescents (particularly young women) to display the signs of apparently promiscuous sexual behaviour as a result of depression. If not addressed at an early stage this can continue into adulthood with harmful, regrettable and painful results whose consequences will be present long after the one-night stand has been forgotten.

The motive is not essentially predatory. In some cases it is a deliberate tactic to shock, to shock parents or relatives or *somebody* into taking them seriously but it can also be a reaction against the personal sense of worthlessness they feel. Not valuing themselves as people they have no incentive to value their bodies either. Rather like eating disorders such as anorexia and bulimia, indiscriminate sexual activity is often a manifestation of lack of self-esteem and not infrequently a plaintive cry to be looked after, loved and cared for. The fleeting comfort of sexual intercourse without emotional commitment persuades the young woman (though men are not immune) that she is wanted – albeit for a night.

A common thread running through addictive behaviour, whether sex, alcohol, or drug related, is the illusory sense of fulfilment it offers. While it lasts the solace such addiction provides is real enough but the temporary high, by its very nature, must inevitably pass which in turn may well serve only to deepen the depressive void such behaviour strives to fill in the first place.

* * *

Beginning with the *wrong* ways of managing depression may seem a perverse starting point. But that is because, although wrong, they are perfectly natural, almost positive, reactions to life's hard knocks. It is as if, in the face of the perceived awfulness of existence, the addictive personality has said, 'Better to get through life *somehow* than to throw in the towel.' The fact that the means chosen are flawed and misguided does not necessarily invalidate the impulse for survival.

Look at the down-and-outs in any city centre nowadays, assailed, with every passing day, by homelessness, illness, loneliness, anxiety, hunger and cold. Is it any wonder they take to the bottle, the needle and cigarettes merely to get by? And should anyone blame them for doing all the wrong things for some of the right reasons? To a world gone haywire, madness itself may sometimes seem the sanest response.

But to most of us sanity and peace of mind are preferable. As Dr Pidd has said, most people do not enjoy being depressed. One of the aims of this chapter is to enable those who have recognised their depression to find for themselves a way out of it and, consequently, to discover a way back to the source of mental well-being.

In this context the experiences of those rootless inner-city destitutes may seem an irrelevance. Not so. They represent merely the extreme end of the scale of human misery for most of us in the West. (Of course, if we were to compare it to the misery of life elsewhere such an experience might not seem extreme at all. Think of the trauma of displacement and civil war in Bosnia, for example, of the sheer bowel-churning savagery that befell Rwanda, or of the desensitising attrition of drought and famine in sub-Saharan Africa. And pause. But the emotional impact of such events is not for discussion here and assessing what depression such chronic horrors will visit on those who have witnessed them is way beyond the scope of this book.) For the moment, suffice to say that between the extremes of human misery and the extremes of human joy there is the 'ordinary' world of human experience which is the one most of us are familiar with and which is the one we shall now consider. In other words 'the heart-ache and the thousand natural shocks that flesh is heir to' of Shakespeare's Hamlet are more than enough for us to be getting on with for the moment.

Even at the best of times life is hard enough. And the thing about it is that it never stops coming at us. A man named Elbert Hubbard defined life as 'one damned thing after another'. Now, in the normal course of events, dealing with each incident as it comes along is what we do without thinking. But when, for whatever reason, we find the healthy balance of our minds upset, coping with what life has to throw at us is that much more difficult. It is then that depression may set in.

Research has been done by two American doctors, Holmes and Rahe, into so-called 'life events' and the corresponding stress these are likely to induce. It is worth looking at the implications of such findings in some detail.

At the top of the list of events which are likely to provoke the greatest stress is bereavement. On this particular scale the loss of a husband or wife is followed closely by divorce or marital separation, a jail term, the death of a close family member, personal injury or illness, marriage, the loss of a job and moving house. All of these, it is claimed, deliver the **highest** levels of stress.

In the next category are those events delivering a **high** stress level. These are marital reconciliation, retirement, serious illness of a family member, pregnancy, sexual difficulties, a new child, a change of job, financial problems and the death of a close friend.

In category three come events producing **moderate** stress levels. These include family arguments, a large mortgage, legal action over debt, a change in responsibilities at work, a son or daughter leaving home, trouble with one's in-laws, outstanding personal achievement, a wife (sic) beginning or stopping work, a change in living conditions, a revision of personal habits, trouble with the boss.

The final category lists the **low** stressors which include a change in working hours or conditions, a change in schools, a change in recreation patterns, a change in church or social activities, a small mortgage or loan, a change in sleeping habits, a change in contact with the family, holidays, Christmas, and minor violations of the law.

Such observations are useful but they do not, in themselves, tell us much about depression. Take bereavement, for example, which is at the top of the list. Some people come through it, others do not. To most of us it will produce great sadness. But sadness is not depression.

Sadness, which is the quite proper reaction to death, illness, separation or loss, may not be a pleasant experience but neither is it unhealthy. Sadness can make us more compassionate, more tolerant, more forgiving and more understanding. It is a positive emotion which can lead to wisdom and acceptance.

As we look through the photograph album in middle or old age we may shed a tear at what has been lost over the years; we may wistfully think back to what was and is no longer, or to what might have been if only we had taken a different course. But the sadness which accompanies such sorrowful introspection does not close our eyes to the future, to the promise held out by children, friends and family when tomorrow dawns. Sadness does not prevent us from doing other things.

Depression is not like that. It is a windowless prison enclosing us in an infernal present which obliterates all promise of tomorrow and invalidates the comforts of yesterday. It is debilitating and life-rejecting.

Why bereavement provokes sadness in some and depression in others has still not been conclusively resolved. Furthermore, why moving house (or, indeed, any of the other life events) should be a trigger for depression is still unclear. 'Of course,' says Dr Pidd, 'you can hypothesise about why moving house should cause such problems. You are uprooting things, leaving memories behind. And then there is the uncertainty, both of making new relationships and of coping financially.'

For many people, of course, such uncertainties are offset by the excitement and exhilaration of moving on. For them, buying a new house is a distinctly positive life event which is not associated with depression at all. Why should this be? Sally Pidd cannot supply an answer, although she knows from clinical experience that it sometimes *is* accompanied by depression. 'I have a patient who has had three severe episodes of depression over the years I have known her,' she recalls, 'and they have all been associated, if not with actually moving house, then, at least with major renovations in the home – having a new kitchen fitted or roofing work done.'

What Dr Pidd has to do is tease out of the situation just how much is 'understandable' depression and how much might be attributable to a biological cause which medication may be able to treat. This is not to say that anti-depressants are to be prescribed with every visit to the estate agent or the DIY store. Far from it, because life events are not necessarily agents of depression in themselves. What they can do, however, is act as triggers which, in combination with other factors, can provoke severe downturns in mood and mental well-being.

But if we accept for a moment the rather flippant definition of life as 'one damned thing after another', then it follows that *everything* we experience (from a stubbed toe to nuclear war) is a life event and just as likely to affect us, to a greater or lesser degree, as anything else.

Professor George Brown, who has studied depression for much of his professional life, puts it as follows: 'The brain is a highly complex organ which is capable of a series of sometimes contradictory responses. An objectively narrow range of experiences is capable of bringing about depression in some, while comparatively intense experiences in others do not have the same effect.'

He gives an example. On the day I contacted him he had just received a letter which was mildly critical of something he had written. The text he had sent for inclusion in a particular journal had been read by the commissioning editor who, in turn, had written back to say that this was not exactly what he had expected. There had clearly been a crossed wire somewhere in the communication. However, Professor Brown was honest enough to admit to himself and to me that he had found that receipt of the letter had projected him into a mood somewhere between irritation and disappointment. In other words, the letter was a life event capable, under the right constellation of moods, circumstances, and other life events of altering the way in which he felt. It did not trigger a depressive attack in him but a similar rebuff might have done so in others.

Or take this account of a dual event (bereavement and the enforced vacating of the family home) which was to be the prelude to a lengthy period of depression culminating in marital separation and, eventually, divorce.

6 Dad's death was bad enough. I hadn't bargained for the sadness of letting go of the house as well. After all, it was just a red-brick council house like every other on the estate. Four walls and a roof rented from the corporation for one lifetime. With no primogeniture. Outwardly, not much of a family seat at all. But it had a history. Forty-two years of it, for the record. And, though it wasn't something Pevsner would have thought worth a detour, I miss it.

Permanence and possession are illusions built into every council property. Sooner or later someone else will move into what you have always called "your" house. In August last year, when my father died, I had three weeks to get things ready for new tenants to move into "ours".

And with that, the house where I had played, slept, studied, laughed, cried, got sick, got well, fretted, panicked, fallen in love, and felt secure was prepared to change owners for the first time in its existence. It was hard.

On my last day there I stepped inside the shell that had housed three lives to find, of course, that all trace of them had gone. In the hall, no holiday trunk for dispatch to Ramsgate; in the kitchen, no pasting board for table tennis; no library books, no evening paper, no French homework, no Meccano. Upstairs, no smell of Mum's talc or Dad's cigarettes.

True, there were memorials in the garden. The apple pip I had stuck into a tub of dirt 30 odd years ago was now a tree. The vine my father had got from God knows where still had its grapes (though not for harvest this year). The slabs of privet which had cushioned an out-of-control Hillman in 1959 were as vigorous as ever. Mature shrubs linked past to future via a present which was now excluding me. It was time to go. As a matter of fact, I had no choice. The new tenants would be arriving soon and I had to be gone.

Clearing out had been a sadness and a sweat. The best of the furniture went to family and friends. The best of the rest to neighbours and the house-clearance people. The rest, suddenly pathetic in the summer heat, hauled into the garden ready for the tip. Carpets were torn up, shelves unscrewed, Dad's bits of plywood, which had shielded the kitchen sink provisionally for four decades, were ripped out and dumped publicly in the skip outside.

That left just the house – as bare as it had been on the day my parents had taken occupation; as bare as it had to be for the "void squad" not to charge for clearance. A bare house which did not belong to me though I had belonged to it for so long.

Unannounced and angelic, four neighbours had turned up to help. Mary made tea and Dora swept while Charlie and George manhandled furniture that had not been moved for years. Having paid their respects to my father it was as if they were now saying farewell to a house which had aged and altered alongside their own.

When all was done I made a last solitary tour, seriously expecting to hear a groan or a sigh from rooms that were giving up possession after all this time. But there was nothing. I took my leave in silence aware that part of my life had come to an end. This once familiar road was history, a now strangely unfamiliar place. And how could this be my home town any more when I had no home there to go to? **'**

Terry, 45. Manchester

Even the slightest experiences can prompt severe reactions in people. Dr Sally Pidd has another example. She was treating a woman for depression and had managed to get her particular condition under control. Bumping into her in the out-patients' department of the hospital she was able to exchange the normal courtesies of the 'Hello, how are things going?' variety, without engaging in a deep analysis of the woman's medical situation. In other words, because her condition was responding well to treatment the patient was behaving as any other person would, and was content to engage with Dr Pidd on a casual level. Then one day, in slightly more of a hurry than usual, Dr Pidd encountered her in the hospital and, while she did not ignore her, she failed to say the cheery 'hello' in quite the same way and, as Dr Pidd puts it, 'That was enough to set her off. She must have done something to upset me. Why was I not taking an interest in her? What had she done? etc, etc.' The fact is that the impact of some events cannot be predicted in advance. So the stress table based on them can only be a guide.

Take Steve's experience. He is enjoying a period of calm and contentment now that he has his depression under control with a combination of anti-depressants and group therapy.

' I've been living with depression for three years now. I felt as if I was going barmy on my own terms basically. I thought it was the sort of thing that only happened to other people. The odd thing is that nothing had happened to provoke it. No parents dying. Nothing dramatic. **'**

What do these apparently contradictory accounts have to say to anyone prone to depression? Well, they say this. Scan the list of life events by all means. If you are in the midst of bereavement or unemployment, if your partner has just been arrested by the police, if your bills are mounting up, if your children have fled the nest for university, if you have received your gold watch for loyal service and are now wondering 'what next?' or whatever disruptive event you are going through, **be prepared** for a change of mood. **Expect** to feel different. Forewarned you can then recognise that a downturn in mood is likely to occur and get yourself ready to take evasive or self-protective action.

You might do the following, for instance:

- Let family and friends know some change is possible in your moods and ask them to be patient.
- Reschedule other potentially disruptive events so as to avoid a form of emotional overload.
- Regularise your sleeping pattern and try to get some rest in advance.
- Delegate or postpone the task of building that room extension.
- Reinstate the healthy-eating plan and the exercise programme you recently shelved.

But, and it is quite a significant but, retirement and Christmas may have come and gone, or you may have taken out a small loan or fallen out with your in-laws with absolutely no ill effect at all. But another incident occurs (say, the Channel Tunnel rail link is planned for the bottom of your garden) and it knocks you for six.

Simon Armson of The Samaritans says that predicting possible depressive bouts is a feature of self-knowledge. Those worst placed to spot depression coming (and so to take evasive action), he says, may be those whose awareness of themselves is deficient. 'What is the nature of the stable state of a person?', he wonders. 'And, indeed, how stable is stable? You may have a person who is superficially in control of life – they have a sound, stable relationship, know what they're doing, have a lovely family, and a good job and so on. But under that veneer of so-called normality may lurk varying degrees of (as yet) unactivated abnormality – whether in the form of a predisposition towards anxiety, a lack of confidence, or of self-worth, or feelings of inferiority.'

When a life event comes along and removes one level of that veneer of stability (the job goes, a husband or wife has an affair, the house is burgled or whatever) then feelings and emotional weaknesses which were once beneath the surface and unrecognised are sometimes painfully exposed. A confluence of such life events can provoke reactive depression which may be all the more intense for being unexpected.

Simon Armson recommends early self-appraisal, a sort of emotional audit, as a preventive measure. 'It's worth knowing where your Achilles heel is,' he says, 'so first of all get to know yourself. Know where there are likely to be pressure points and where points of anxiety are likely to arise. If you know in advance where the tension could occur you can then say, "OK, that's something I recognise I'm going to have to give time and energy to." I'm not suggesting we become navel-contemplating, self-indulgent, introspective people but just that we increase our knowledge of the kind of person we really are. It could be said that the ultimate extension of this is that we all undergo psycho-analysis. But I'm not saying that at all. What I am saying is that we, as individuals, take note of the things that cause us to feel different emotions. What makes you feel sad? What makes you feel angry? What makes you feel ashamed? What makes you feel happy?

'By developing this sort of self-awareness the chances of your being able to anticipate difficulties are greatly improved. It's like budgeting your weekly needs. You know how much you will have to spend on food, on heating, on rent and so on. And you know how much you have coming into the house. There's almost the need for an *emotional* budgeting process. You have to know what demands are likely to be made on you and what resources you have to be able to cope with them. And if that means you are going to have to spend two weeks doing something rather than one, then so be it. Better that than emotional overload.'

Conversely, those *in* depression can sometimes be induced, if not to get out of it, at least to endure or deal with it in a satisfactory way by recognising an already existing pattern behind it. Dr Pidd, for example, has treated patients with recurrent mood swings: 'The classic ones will be people who have seasonal mood swings,' she says, 'not necessarily Seasonal Affective Disorder, which is all the rage at the moment, but people who are definitely down in the winter and who then perk up in the spring. I'm treating someone who can almost trade on that. She knows that the summers are going to be fine. But as the year wears on so her mood goes down. But she says to herself, "If I can just see past Christmas in the depressed state, then I'll be all right from then on."'

Knowing that a depression will not last for ever is undoubtedly helpful to a sufferer. The problem is that for some, no matter how much they are told that it will *not* last for ever, they are incapable of accepting it. The depression has them so completely in its airtight bell jar that no breath of comfort from the outside world can be admitted.

For others, however, strategies can be developed to keep the worst of the attacks at bay. Dr Pidd refers back to the patient whose depressions have so far lasted three years at a time (a good two years more than most of us would probably feel able to cope with, but he has got by!). The patient in question is a highly gifted scientist whose output when he was well was compensation enough for those lengthy periods when he was not. 'This man is clinging on to the fact that his depressions have never lasted longer than three years,' says Dr Pidd, 'so in a sense he's counting the days.' Such fortitude may be beyond most of us but he is able to accept it so, with understanding and flexible employers, this routine has worked well for him over the years.

To be reminded that a depression will run a fixed course can be very useful and Dr Pidd employs such strategies to minimise the worst of its effects. So, in the case of the woman whose depression comes on every time there is some sort of disruption in the house, she reminds her of the pattern her illness has taken so far. She has also enlisted the help of her patient's supportive husband who has proved to be a wonderful ally. He, too, will say, 'Look, you've been like this before and it has got better in the past. It will get better in the future.'

Such reassurance may need to be given time and time again (sometimes in inverse proportion to its apparent effectiveness) but the cumulative, almost ritualistic, effect of repetition will help whatever cognitive processes are functioning at the time. That is to say, if you keep on saying it, it may just (just) get through in the end. It may not be guaranteed, of course, but what *is* guaranteed is this: if you don't, it won't.

Dr Pidd also employs a number of very practical exercises which can reinforce other treatments she is administering at the time. For example, over long experience she has noticed that patients, when coming out of depression, have relapses, ups and downs, a few good days followed by a couple of serious reverses. Often these patients will get despondent, thinking that just when they thought they were beginning to see the light the shutters start to come down.

Under these circumstances she suggests that they write a little card and put it on the mantelpiece. On it she suggests they write: 'I may be depressed today but I wasn't yesterday. And I won't be tomorrow.' She will often encourage them to keep diaries or notebooks in which they make a point of jotting down the positive things they have done every day. Both these strategies have one distinct advantage. There is objective, printed evidence of mood variations and, confronted with it, a depressive will have to accept it at some level of his or her consciousness. What individuals then choose (or are able) to do with this information may vary. In the short term the revelation may produce no visible results at all; it may even be challenged at a subsequent date and denounced as worthless. But the fact remains that objective evidence exists of some sort of improvement over time and, lodged in the brain, this evidence may yet be deployed at a crucial moment to help the sufferer out of the pit.

Dr Pidd uses other practical methods, too. One woman she used to see had become very physically run down by her depression, something which was reflected in the lack of care she took about her personal appearance. Every time she appeared in the out-patients' clinic, for example, she would be wearing the same clothes. One afternoon, Dr Pidd decided to mention it – not in a spirit or tone of criticism, merely as a point of observable fact.

'The thing is,' said the patient, 'I can't choose what to wear in the morning.'

'Why not try this,' replied Dr Pidd. 'Why not lay a new set of clothes out on the bed in the evening so that all you have to do in the morning is put them on?'

What Dr Pidd knew was that, in common with many depressives, the morning was her patient's worst time. This was when despondency was at its height and when everyday decisions were next to impossible to make.

The patient gave it a try. And, having seen that it worked once, tried it again. An old, essentially negative pattern had been broken and a new, more positive one had taken its place. When Dr Pidd and her patient next talked on the phone a mundane topic of conversation could be pursued.

'What are you wearing?' she would ask.

'Oh, a red sweater . . .' or whatever, or whatever – the very ordinariness of the conversation being a positive indication that her patient was back again in the everyday, 'normal' world. The point is obvious. Having been encouraged to do something positive (lay out the next day's wardrobe) in the evening when she was feeling well, she was able to get her emotional bank account into credit. In the morning, when her emotional reserves were low (and even deciding whether to wear tights or not was beyond her) she could trade on the effort made the night before and, at no extra emotional effort to herself, could start the day in a better frame of mind.

The same basic tactic can be used to achieve different goals. So, in the evening you could:

- Lay out the breakfast things for the next day. Put the tea bag in the pot and the cereal in the bowl. Fill the kettle.
- Pack your briefcase or load up your handbag with all you will need tomorrow. This way you avoid the agony of decision and have the reserves for the day.
- Make out a list of achievable goals. List five of them, (go to the post office, take in dry cleaning, plant seeds, change light bulb, write letter, or whatever) and aim to do at least two. If you do, congratulate yourself. If you don't, stay calm and try again tomorrow.
- Look back on the day and list the things that have given you pleasure or satisfaction. Keep them to hand and consult them when things are going badly.

- Say goodnight to your partner. If alone, say goodnight to yourself.
- Keep a radio and a torch by the bed.

As Dr Pidd puts it, 'It's a question of making tasks simple enough so that people feel they've made some headway. There's nothing worse than setting people a task they can't do. That just increases their sense of failure. So, in the case of my patient with the red sweater, it would have been pointless suggesting that she make a trip to the local shops because she lives in a village. That would have meant checking the times of the bus, queuing up, then doing the same for the return trip – far too big a step. So I made the task easier and suggested a "simple" change of clothing. And she did actually feel better for it.'

❛ You have to work towards the recovery of self-esteem. This is crucial. You have to survive from day to day. There's absolutely no point in looking ten years ahead. I couldn't possibly think about what the future would be like in ten days time, let alone ten years. At its worst you just have to tell yourself to survive for one more day, and one more day, and one more day. ❜

Paul Lanham

Dr Pidd recalls another patient, highly talented but unable to work for long periods because of depression. He was an intelligent man who took an abstract interest in his own condition and, viewing it as a puzzle to be solved, was happy to intellectualise his problem. (One of the many ironies about depression is that reading up on your condition, consulting all the tomes and papers written on it does not automatically help you beat it. It may give you a fascinating insight into your condition – but it won't necessarily get you out of bed in the morning.) Anyway, this patient was quite taken by some research study that had been carried out with a group of depressives who had been encouraged to perform a dull, repetitive task. In their case they were put in a room with dozens of wooden blocks. Then they were given a piece of sandpaper each and told to sand down the blocks one after the other.

The idea behind the experiment was to get people to express some emotion, something which people in the depressed state find very hard to do. As each person had finished the tedious business of sanding a block, a new block was handed over to be sanded again, followed by another, and another until the patient said a more or less acceptable version of, 'Hang on a minute. I've had enough of this' and walked out. The exercise had been deliberately planned with the intention of harnessing the emotion of irritation as a positive means of jolting him or her out of a flat inexpressive mood.

Armed with this finding Dr Pidd discussed with her patient possible ways of employing the technique. He listened and nodded and was clearly quite taken with the idea. But, to show that Dr Pidd is human and has *her* failures, too, he could not be persuaded. 'He just wouldn't bite on it,' she remembers. But perhaps others can!

What this story and the research with the wooden blocks trade on is that anger, when directed positively, can be beneficial. When it is uncontrolled and negative its effects can be profoundly destructive. When it is not expressed at all, but rather turned in on a person, anger can be self-destructive. In a significant number of cases depression is a feature of anger turned in on itself.

Getting to know the roots of your own anger may be best achieved in conjunction with a counsellor or therapist who may be able to lead you back through formative (usually childhood) experiences to discover whether any unresolved anger has contributed to the state you are in. Finding a therapist involves some effort. The first place for advice is, as usual, your already overworked GP. It may be possible to have a course of therapy on the NHS but it is more likely that you will have to pay (as a rough guide at the time of writing) between £20 and £50 for a one-hour session with a private psychotherapist.

A word of warning. In addition to costing time and money, consulting a therapist involves a degree of risk. There are undoubtedly many untrained or unsympathetic therapists out there who are capable of doing great harm – just as there are many wise counsellors who are prepared to help you to explore the nature of your depressed condition.

When deciding who – if anyone – you should see, remember:

1 Consulting a therapist is not obligatory.
2 A recommendation from someone whom you trust is a good start.
3 Ask the therapist as many questions as you wish to get an idea of what you can expect.
4 You should feel comfortable and secure in his or her presence.
5 You can terminate the treatment at any time.
6 Trust your instincts and be prepared to exercise your freedom to walk away.

Horror stories abound about mind manipulation and control, about unprincipled charlatans who are there to take advantage of you financially and sexually, of inexperienced bunglers who lead you up blind alleys and off beaten tracks. Take note. Such horror stories are true.

If, however, you are fortunate enough to encounter a wise and trustworthy practitioner – he or she may be a psychiatrist, a psychologist, a psychotherapist or a trained counsellor – then your sessions will be wholesome and healing. Together, with no fear of embarrassment or shame, you can share your innermost anxieties and experiences. The process will lead towards an understanding of how and why you have arrived at where you are. It may be painful at times (and there will be many tears as you relive deep hurts and experiences you have kept hidden for a lifetime) but the end product is your well-being. This is how one woman describes her experience:

> ❝ Seven years ago I was suffering from severe depression. I could not sleep and kept bursting into tears without knowing why. All day I was completely exhausted. Now, after seven years of psychotherapy I am able to enjoy life. My psychotherapist explained to me that I was repressing feelings of anger. This caused my tiredness. Gradually I realised I was angry with the most important people in my life. I love my parents and I did not want to admit that they had neglected me emotionally.

At home I was never allowed to express my anger so I used a lot of energy "blocking it out". My father had a bad heart so I was afraid to be angry with him in case it made him ill. His first wife had died leaving three young children. I was forbidden to be angry with them when they upset me, because they had lost their mother so young. I was the "lucky" one because I had my mother but I was never accepted by my half-siblings.

It took me many years to realise how much I had been rejected by those I love most. When I stopped blocking out the pain, I became far less tired. My psychotherapy took so long because I did not often have the courage to talk about my past. Instead, I would talk about the insignificant problems of the past week. For example, if a shop assistant was rude to me, I would be devastated and the incident would be blown out of all proportion. By focusing on the shop assistant I would try to escape from the acute pain of my childhood rejections.

All my life I felt that I had a "voice" inside me, criticising everything I did, so I had no self-confidence. During my therapy I discovered that this voice came from my close family and I have stopped listening to it. Instead I have learnt to love myself and develop my talents.

Although I found psychotherapy painful, my psychotherapist was extremely supportive. She "held my hand" until I came to terms with my past. Now I feel able to put the past behind me and enjoy the second half of my life. There IS light at the end of the tunnel and it is well worth making the journey. **'**

Daphne

The therapy is not magic. The therapist has no wand or potion to make it all better. Your active cooperation and consent are vital components. Even if the therapy is successful it may not succeed completely but, at its best, it will give you strength and power over your own life. It will build you up and persuade you, at every turn, of your own worth. It will not transform you into superman or superwoman but again, at its best, it will enable you to find your true self and, in the process, an exhilarating sense of liberation.

Most of what it achieves it does *with* you: but if it does anything *for* you it is this; it asks you about the membership card you were given at birth. Without anger or irritation it gently wonders why you might have lost it, or failed to renew it over the years. And, accepting every one of your more or less persuasive excuses, it patiently writes you out a new one and says, 'Here. Welcome back to the human race.'

* * *

Whether you are taking medication or having therapy to treat your depression, or whether you are doing both ('pills for the symptoms, talk for the problem') the indispensable component in all this is you.

There are certain things you can do which, it is generally agreed, produce beneficial results. These things will not automatically cure the depression but they may either relieve some of the symptoms or contribute to a greater sense of inner resilience which will give you the strength to carry on. Where to begin?

If you turn back to the introduction to this book and read again the honest account by Isabelle of a randomly chosen 12-day period during which she kept a diary of her moods, one recurrent theme hits you between the eyes. Fatigue.

It features in every single entry of Isabelle's diary and is something with which anyone who has suffered from depression will be familiar. Chronic, sapping fatigue. Bone-weary tiredness which undermines your every good intention and denies you the opportunity of taking part in what the world has to offer.

You can't lift a finger. You can't read a book because you can't summon the energy even to turn the page. It is the fatigue that confined Nick, the writer, to five months in bed. Sure, he got up to go to the lavatory. But afterwards he returned to the bed. His girlfriend brought him meals in bed, meals which he rarely ate. He simply stayed in bed. For five months.

This is how he describes it now:

❝I was shaking all over. My brain seemed to have blacked out. I had lost all contact with the outside world and I was completely engulfed in what was going on inside me. If I could have pressed a button to end it all I would have done. But I wasn't even capable of getting that together. ❞

But one of the crueller ironies of the depressed condition is that sleep does not always bring rest. Or, more correctly, the wrong kind of sleep does not bring rest. And because of the disrupted sleep patterns that many depressives undergo, the wrong kind of sleep is exactly what most of them experience.

Providing someone with a good night's sleep, therefore, can be a useful first step. 'If you have the sort of depression which is the product of what I would call understandable misery,' says Dr Pidd, 'pills won't do anything. Unless, that is, you can see a symptomatic benefit. Lots of people going through miserable patches in their lives don't sleep very well. Quite a lot of anti-depressants contain a sedative which will also help them to sleep. And even if you don't do anything else people will feel a bit better for taking them.'

This is, of course, a short-hand account of what is an extremely complex process. Sleeping pills of any kind are not a permanent solution to a problem and some are known to have undesirable side-effects – a feeling of tiredness or irritability the next day, for example. Not only that, their effectiveness tends to diminish with overuse which, in turn, may prompt people to take increasing doses and expose themselves to dependency.

The prescription of any medication will have to be left to the skill and experience of professionals but the principle, under the correct conditions, still applies. Namely, that if it is possible to get one symptom under control (say, the sleeplessness) then the patient is in a better frame of mind (and body) to respond more successfully to the next stage of treatment.

In some cases depression can be brought on by extreme tiredness, overwork or stress. Paul Lanham believes that overwork was responsible for precipitating his own condition several years ago. 'I was trying too hard,' he says now. 'It goes back to school. I had to succeed at whatever I did. During my first curacy I worked and worked and worked. I remember someone asking me at an interview what I would do if the parish started slipping. And I said, "Work harder". When people say they're busy I always look at things from the other end. I say, "I've got 168 hours in the week to fill." ' So, ignoring all the danger signs, Paul pushed himself more and more. Not to have done, he says, would have meant 'failing myself and failing God'.

While Paul may well have been doing lots of things in the parish he was actually exhausting himself, setting the stage for a bout of mental illness and contributing to the condition which was ultimately to bring about his premature retirement at the age of 44. In the end early retirement meant he was deprived of the very thing he loved – the ministry – which in turn only increased his depression.

While medication, under strict medical supervision, may help people to get the rest they need, there are a number of self-help techniques which can be practised perfectly safely by those who have an aversion to pills or who feel that such chemical intervention is inappropriate for them. The Royal College of Psychiatrists, for example, has some very simple advice for those trying to get a good night's sleep:

1　Don't go without sleep for a long time. Keep to a regular pattern of sleep and waking whether you are tired or not.
2　Make sure that your bed and bedroom are comfortable – not too hot, too cold or too noisy.
3　Take moderate amounts of exercise such as walking or swimming.
4　Cut down or stop drinking tea or coffee in the evening. Try a milky drink before going to bed.
5　Don't drink a lot of alcohol. It may help you fall asleep, but it will almost certainly make you wake through the night.
6　Don't eat or drink a lot late at night. Try to have an evening meal early rather than late.
7　If you have had a bad night, resist the temptation to sleep the next day. It will make it harder to go to sleep the next night.
8　Try to relax properly before going to bed. Your doctor may be able to recommend a helpful relaxation tape.
9　If something is troubling you and there is nothing you can do about it at that particular moment, try writing it down before you go to bed. Then tell yourself you can deal with it tomorrow.
10　If you can't sleep don't lie there worrying about it. Get up and do something you find relaxing like reading, watching television, or listening to quiet music.

In the severely depressed state even some of these simple rec-
ommendations may be beyond you. In which case, do what you
can and do not be troubled by what you can't.

Frequently, depression is accompanied by panic attacks and
anxiety. Panic used to be thought of as a feature of anxiety but
some doctors have now classified it as a separate disorder which
they treat with chemical means. Anxiety is a form of over-
arousal which manifests itself often in a highly physical way.
Take Isabelle's experience, for example:

> 6 The anxiety makes me feel very frightened. My heart starts
> beating too fast and I really feel I'm going to have some kind
> of heart attack. I start hyperventilating and get cold but
> sweaty at the same time and I can't stop shaking. And then I
> panic about panicking which makes me more and more
> afraid. I feel I'm going to black out. 9

Dr Pidd has seen the symptoms before. 'People who show anxiety have over-arousal of the autonomic nervous system. So
people sweat, they get palpitations, go hot and cold; their
breathing gets very rapid and they develop tightness of the
chest. Those feelings then often engender the psychic sensation
of panic because you think something awful is about to happen
– impending doom or a heart attack. Sometimes people get
the sense of panic without all the other associated anxiety
symptoms but usually panic attacks are associated with all the
physical accompaniments of anxiety.'

But there is good news. 'It's relatively easy to teach people to
control those by non-chemical means – relaxation techniques,
yoga, and things like that. Most of the symptoms are physical
and if you get the physical symptoms under control, the psychological ones come under control as well.'

Dr André Tylee concedes that anxiety is a condition separate
from depression but very often a patient will present mixed
anxiety and depression so that it is very difficult, if the condition
has been left undiagnosed for some time, to know where the
anxiety leaves off and the depression begins. People can be
anxious, for example, without being depressed – those with
phobias often fall into this category – but over time the restric-

tions that the anxiety has brought to bear on their lives may be more than sufficient to induce mild, moderate, or severe depression.

He regularly treats patients with overlapping states of anxiety, panic, stress and depression and is able, using some of the therapists on hand in the practice, to train them in a number of self-help methods to reduce the tension involved. The aim here, he says, is to complement whatever treatment he is giving them at the time. 'The stress management classes we run work very well for certain people. One of the reasons they work is that the participants are in a group of eight or nine people and they can get support from each other. Many then go on to form their own independent networks of self-help groups which put into effect outside the surgery the techniques they have learnt inside it.'

There are two basic approaches to reducing stress. The first is to reduce or to avoid stressful experiences. And the second is to manage the stress that unavoidable experiences generate.

Method one, says Dr Tylee, may involve the following:

- **Time management**. Plan your day or your week in advance to spread the load of work and domestic or family pressure evenly. Avoid deferring tasks, chores, and responsibilities until the last minute. Do what can be done as soon as possible so as to avoid the inevitable log jam and resultant emotional overload.
- **Realistic self-appraisal**. Don't say 'Yes' to everything. Take on only those commitments you know you are going to be able to fulfil. Don't feel guilty that you cannot do everything. If overstress induces illness you may find yourself unable to do anything at all over an extended period of time. Look after yourself.
- **Delegation**. Accept that there are some things that you as an individual will not be able to do unaided. Develop the confidence to know that others can do aspects of your work just as well as you. Begin to get used to the uncomfortable truth that no one is indispensable.
- **Accepting limitations**. Pushing ourselves that little bit further is the stuff of achievement and progress. It properly fuels our

ambition and rightly gives us satisfaction. But in times of
stress and crisis it may be wise, temporarily at least, to scale
down your aspirations. Don't make yourself ill by constantly
pushing yourself beyond your natural limits.
• **Accepting help**. Avoid the feeling that you have to be self-
sufficient at all times. Just as you can support others, accept
that others can support you. Develop networks of family and
friends who can help you lighten your load.

Method two involves *dealing with* stress caused by things (or
people) you cannot change or avoid.

'Let's say you have a really unpleasant boss, for example,'
says Dr Tylee. 'Clearly you can't get rid of the boss. But what
you can do is learn to cope with the situation. You might need to
go to the loo for five minutes or find a room where you can be
quiet for a moment. Taking deep breaths helps in these circumstances, as does relaxing your muscles. You might do a bit of
"creative visualisation" which is a form of mild self-hypnosis
which could involve picturing yourself on a beach, say, or imagining yourself somewhere else. You put yourself in a relaxed
state of mind and then go back and join the fray.'

'People with anxiety will very often benefit from relaxation
techniques. Deep breaths and what's called diaphragmatic
breathing will help. This involves pushing the diaphragm down
to get more air into the lungs, which increases the level of
oxygen in your blood which in turn has a relaxing effect.
Learning to relax your muscles progressively also helps.'

Putting effort into relaxing may seem an odd paradox. But, in
the increasingly frenetic and artificial world in which we all live,
many of us have lost the natural mechanisms that once kept the
proper balance between stress and its resolution. At its most
basic (and exaggerated): the sabre-toothed tiger roared and our
caveman ancestor made a run for it, or fought it off with a spear.
In so doing the adrenaline levels which were generated by the
tiger, were dispersed by the getaway or the fight.

Nowadays, stress levels are generated just as effectively by
the computer screen or by the fact that the lift to your tenth floor
flat is out of order. But the possibilities of siphoning off that

adrenaline are much more reduced as a result of our sedentary lives. What we are much more likely to do in order to seek temporary relief from stress is to drink, smoke, or over-eat which, in the long term, only add to the problem.

Exercise, of course, is the classic way to compromise. And even moderate amounts of exercise have been shown not only to reduce stress levels but also to have a direct bearing on mood. Common sense suggests that going for a walk will 'take your mind off things' and 'get you out of yourself' but very often this kind of remark is the last thing a depressed person wants to hear. In the severe state, depression acts like a filter, sucking out all the good sense and good intention of a piece of advice and leaving only a husk of irritating words.

If a depressed person knows in advance that taking exercise *is a clinically proved way of altering the metabolism* (rather than cracker-barrel wish fulfilment) then he or she may be inclined to reach for it as a solution when the worst of the depression lifts. Exercise stimulates the production of endorphins in the body (these are chemicals containing minute quantities of natural morphine). When released into the system, endorphins produce an increased sense of well-being which is a natural way of breaking into the depressed mood and lightening it.

Ian who, at 36, is able to go in for the more energetic sports is a staunch advocate:

> 6 Over the years I've relied a lot on sports and exercise to get me out of the depressions. I play a lot of badminton and that has helped. But it was a two-edged thing because over the years I improved and learnt things like backhand shots. So that meant that I didn't have to dash around the court so much – which meant I didn't get the endorphin rush. Even so I do feel better after exercise – as long as it's rigorous. 9

Exercise need not be too rigorous, of course, and in many cases taking up an energetic sport will be unwise. It is important to match your exercise to your age and general level of fitness. Exchanging depression for a heart attack is a dubious trade off. Walking and swimming are gentle ways to begin any exercise programme. Be sensible about what sports and exercise are within your competence.

Relaxation, which does not involve medication, is another natural way of achieving peace of mind. It also has the advantage that you need not buy funny shorts or hang around in chilly changing rooms.

Basic relaxation need involve no more than the following:

- Find a quiet place where you can be undisturbed for 15 minutes or so.
- Sit comfortably (but don't slouch) on a chair or lie on a hard bed or on the floor out of range of any draughts.
- Let your whole body relax, drooping under the weight of gravity. Do not tense any muscles.
- Slowly close your eyes but resist any temptation to fall asleep.
- Simply breathe slowly and rhythmically, listening to the sound of your own breathing.
- Continue for ten or 20 minutes and repeat twice a day.

If you find this useful, you can then go on to slightly more advanced forms of relaxation – sometimes performed to the accompaniment of a relaxation tape which has been specially composed to calm the senses.

Advanced relaxation

- Choose the same undisturbed spot as in basic relaxation.
- Lie comfortably on the floor.
- With your legs slightly apart and your arms just to the side of your body concentrate on one part of the body in turn.
- Begin with your head. Let it rest on the floor. Don't press it or force it. Merely concentrate on its weight as you surrender all resistance to gravity.
- Move next to your left shoulder. Let it relax and, without exerting any pressure or resistance, let it sag naturally to the floor.
- Next concentrate on your upper arm, elbow and forearm. Each time let this part of your body settle into its natural unresisted place on the floor. Feel the resistance giving way slowly as each section of your body relaxes under its natural weight.

- Continue this process with your hand and fingers on the left side. Then move to the hand and fingers on the right. Make the same journey up the right hand side allowing your lower arm, elbow, upper arm and right shoulder to surrender to their natural weight.
- Begin the journey down the centre of your body imagining all your internal organs settling under their own weight.
- Do the same with the small of your back, your buttocks, thighs, knees, calves and feet.
- When you are quite still (breathing rhythmically all the while) start to listen with increasing degrees of intentness. First listen to the sounds of your breathing, then to the sounds in the room – the creaking of a floorboard, the ticking of a clock. Then listen to the sounds outside the door. A hum from the refrigerator, a dripping tap, a cat padding about the hall. Then listen to sounds outside – the birdsong, an overhead plane, a hum of traffic. Listen to them intently, as you haven't before. Enjoy them as a form of music (some calming, some jarring, notes). Dissect all the component noises which go to make up what you are listening to.
- After ten minutes or so, pull back the focus of your listening, gradually concentrating on the sounds nearer and nearer to you – ending with your breathing.
- Start the journey round your limbs again, this time slowly and gently stirring them back into life. Moving a shoulder, then the parts of your arm, your hand, fingers etc.
- When you have completed the journey slowly stand. Pause for a minute or two to consider the exercise.
- Slowly open your eyes.
- The exercise is over.

Progressive Relaxation is a way, not only of relaxing generally, but of controlling anxiety attacks.

- Lie on a comfortable surface – a sofa, a bed or the floor.
- Work through your body parts as before but, instead of relaxing each part, tense it slowly. Then, after you have tensed and held the tension for a moment, *slowly* release the tension and relax your muscles.

- Work with one side then the next. Tensing and relaxing. When you reach your head you can work on individual facial muscles. Clench your jaw – then relax. Screw your eyes up – then slowly open them. Tense your scalp – then relax.
- Each time feel the sensation of tension. Think to yourself as you hold the position for four or five seconds each time 'this is what tension feels like'. Then relax for ten seconds or so and think 'this is relaxation'.
- After the customary tour round the body stand up *slowly*. And pause, before slowly resuming normal life.

For some, such exercises may seem strange – even eccentric. So it is worth while remembering this. There is no obligation on you to do any of them and if they seem to go against the grain of your personality, so be it. Consider some other activity more in tune with the way you are. Take the dog for a walk, knit (if you can summon the concentration), tidy the garage or whatever. These may all, in the end, have the same therapeutic effect. That said, you might just feel tempted to try one exercise while no one is looking!

Either way, though, the underlying principle is not to brood on the depression but to take an active step to overcome it. This step may not be large but the mere fact that you have taken it will be enough to raise your self-esteem that little bit further and to give you the feeling that you are once again back in control.

One of the worst features of the depressed state is a feeling of being powerless to resist whatever wave of awfulness comes over you next. Becoming an active player in life rather than one of its passive victims is crucial in gaining any renewed sense of well-being. Paul Lanham can testify to the importance of this principle in his own life. After his career in the church came to an end he found himself overwhelmed with depression and from being a man who carried out ten jobs before lunchtime and had another ten planned for the afternoon, he became someone for whom the tiniest chore required an almost superhuman effort.

Paul had to adapt – and he did. Taking the advice of a GP and a psychiatrist (and supported, it has to be said, by a patient, tolerant family) he dutifully wrote lists of tasks to achieve each day and, through sheer determination, forced himself to carry out one of them. He knew in advance that carrying out more than one would be beyond him so he was wise enough to attempt what was within his capacity and not to be further downcast by what he could not achieve.

In this he was putting into practice an important (and, for the depressed, extremely useful) principle developed by the late Bruno Bettelheim in his book, *A Good Enough Parent*. In this book Bettelheim, whose pioneering work in the field of child psychology acquired him a distinguished, if controversial, reputation during his lifetime, contended that, while we all strive for perfection, it is folly to think we can achieve it. Real wisdom, he said, rests in knowing what our limitations are and working creatively within them.

Rearing a child, therefore, a most important human endeavour, was something we assumed we had to do to perfection. We had to get it just right, spot on, every time, all the time. This, Bettelheim argued, was fundamentally misguided. It was an impossible task for any one human being to perform and anyone seriously embarking on this road to perfection would be storing up problems ahead. Far better, he concluded, to be a parent who was *good enough*.

This principle can be transferred to the treatment of depression. Before his illness Paul Lanham was active and productive in a way which would have shamed many a younger man. After his illness he had to accept drastic limitations on his performance. Wisdom lay in the acceptance of his limitations. No longer was he the perfect, all-achieving Paul Lanham of old (which was itself a fiction because his relentless drive had contributed to his breakdown in the first place), instead he was someone capable *enough* of getting by, one step at a time, until he became stronger.

So he accepted the discipline of the daily lists and congratulated himself when he had carried out a set task. 'Self congratulation,' he says now, 'is absolutely basic – even if it's a question of doing only one practical thing a day.' The nature of that 'one thing' per day will be for each individual to decide for himself or herself. It could be as minor as going to the shop for a paper, or putting fresh flowers in the vase. What matters is doing it and reminding yourself at the end of the day that you have done it.

When Paul's depression deepened so, too, did other conditions. In particular he became agoraphobic, fearing to go even small distances alone. And yet, all the time, he concentrated on what he was still good enough at doing. Public speaking, for example, was a skill which came naturally to him so he reminded himself of that at every turn. 'I might have had a speaking engagement five miles up the road at which I was expected to address 200 people,' he says. 'I'd tell myself that I had an enviable talent. Speaking to 200 people, after all, isn't something everybody can do. The fact that I was practically paralysed with fear at the prospect of getting to a spot five miles away was by the by.'

Those who are depressed need not feel that they have to take a course in public speaking to get out of their depression. Countless other possibilities exist, each *good enough* to persuade a sufferer that he or she can get by for a bit longer until the mood lifts.

While you carry out these daily tasks it is as well to remind yourself that you are suffering from a temporary illness. You are not abnormal nor insane. You are depressed – as lots of other people have been in the past. Remember that 95 per cent of those treated for depression recover quickly and, just as they have got better, so, too, will you. Even though, admittedly, it does not always feel like that at the time.

> ❝ The first time I was told it was depression, I convinced myself it would go away and not come back. It did and it was hell. But then it disappeared again. And since then this sane inner voice says to me, "Oh. You've had this before. It'll go. Hang on in." It doesn't always do a lot of good . . . but it's there and it's useful. ❞
>
> *Steve*

Anyone NOT familiar with depression would be well advised to ponder on the sheer courage which underlies so apparently unremarkable a statement.

For someone suffering clinical depression a routine and a

structured day are invaluable. All too often
perceive the world as a series of disjointed an
single experiences devoid of any overall pattern.
present themselves as a chaotic and unstoppable
events, duties and chores which simply cannot be   d.
Establishing a structured routine enables people to make sense
of the turmoil and, to a greater or lesser degree, to tame it.

Dr Desmond Kelly, a psychiatrist working at the Priory
Hospital in London, believes it may be one of the most significant
aspects of recovery and advises patients to try to achieve defined
goals every day. In this way, he says, 'faulty habits can be overcome and more healthy patterns of behaviour re-established'.

Under a general principle of 'Just For Today' he suggests the
following advice:

1 Don't try to solve all life's problems in a day; break difficulties down into small tasks, and make a start by taking a
   small, concrete step each day.
2 Keep your mind and body active; do not retreat to bed, or
   abuse drugs or alcohol; self-pity and isolation will make
   matters worse.
3 Try not to procrastinate but instead resolve each and every
   day to do one thing which you have hitherto avoided doing.
4 Try to be agreeable and courteous to others, because they are
   then likely to reflect your mood and behaviour.
5 Do not criticise or blame others; this is not the time to seek to
   change them but to change yourself.
6 Dress as becomingly as possible, because this will serve to
   increase your sense of well-being and thereby help you to
   regain your self-esteem.
7 Try to do something to help somebody else. This will take
   your mind off your own problems and, by helping others,
   you will be doing a lot to help yourself. Set yourself a
   challenge.
8 Have courage – with faith and help, even the greatest
   problems can be overcome. Try to look for something of
   beauty and to enjoy it; your sense of happiness will then
   slowly return.

9 Accept what cannot be changed and count your blessings, for matters could be a great deal worse. Doing, rather than thinking and brooding, will restore you to health and happiness.

10 Use a stress-reduction method daily such as yoga, a relaxation cassette, meditation, or a favourite piece of music. This will help you to sleep more soundly and make you feel more at peace with the world.

By common consent, taking one day at a time is the best psychological ploy to adopt. Self-preservation needs to be thought of as a well-prepared campaign strategy, a battle plan to beat the foe. True, it is not easy defeating an enemy that has stationed its front line in your head but remember that the enemy *can* be routed. Even if its defeat is not immediate you, at least, can live to fight another day with these appropriate words as your motto: 'What does not kill me makes me strong.'

5

Suicide: Thinking the Unthinkable

On the cover of their booklet on the costs of suicide The Samaritans print a telling photograph. It is of a stone falling into a pond sending ripples to the shore. Some of the ripples are solid, some are faint but all of them move with the same inexorable momentum from the centre out, to break much later, with varying degrees of force, on the waiting shoreline.

The analogy is clear. Long after the stone has disappeared from view the effects of its violent intrusion into the calm surface of the pond continue to be felt. Just as families touched by suicide continue to suffer long after one of their members has taken the irrevocable step of ending his or her life. Clearly suicides have suffered grievously. The peculiar horror of each individual nightmare is beyond our imagining. While we can only guess at its nature we can be sure that the suffering was immense.

That is terrible enough. But the real horror, the really exquisite twist some agent of malevolence has devised is this: that from the pit of a private hell prospective suicides cannot possibly know what horrors they, in their turn, will visit on those who love them most.

What follow are two accounts of lives overshadowed by violent death. Two ordinary families, like the families of the 4,628 individuals in Britain who took their own lives in 1992 (the most recent reliable figure). They represent no one but themselves and yet their grief and their heartache (as well as their anger and their resentment) go some way to hint at the bottomless well of pain this ambivalent act of violence can expose.

* * *

Lorna and her children, Alec and Amy, learnt to live with two
people in their house. One was Tony, the children's father and
Lorna's husband of 16 years; the other was 'horrible Herbert',
the sullen stranger in their midst who looked like Tony but who
behaved quite differently.

Tony had suffered from bouts of depression all his life but
over the years they had got worse. Lorna watched helplessly as
the depressions took hold of him and transformed this normally
lively, outgoing 40-year-old family man into a different person
who would sit in the chair for hours on end vacantly staring into
space and lacking all motivation to do anything.

Strangely enough he was capable of doing his job – lorry
driving – quite well, a skill Lorna ascribes to his ability to put on
a front and to disguise his real feelings outside the house. He
was a popular man at work and a loving family man at home –
until, that is, he became engulfed in his depression and became,
quite simply, a man transformed. At his worst, he would turn
up in the evenings almost spoiling for an argument and in a
state so unpredictable that he scared his daughter. 'We just
didn't know what was going to walk through the door,' says
Lorna.

When the worst of the dark moods descended and cast their
gloom throughout the household Tony's son, Alec, then only 12,
learnt to keep his distance. Once he remembers confronting his
father in the kitchen and, roused to fury, told him to stop shouting at his mum. It was an ugly and upsetting confrontation
which left Alec with a 'jumble of emotions'. Why was his father
shouting so loud? What was Alec doing berating his own father?
How had their once-happy family come to this? More simply:
what was going on? The answer to all these questions, of course,
could be summed up in one word but, although Alec had been
told that his father was ill with depression, he was still too
young to understand the full nature and implications of his
father's condition.

Like the impressionable daughters of Paul Lanham (and like
countless other young children of depressives) Alec was left in
dreadful confusion, in mute, angry, frightened and impotent
bewilderment. Why should he be behaving like this with a

father he loved? Perhaps depressive illness was what all dads had and perhaps he, Alec, was really to blame.

For the sake of the family Lorna gave Tony an ultimatum.'Things got so bad that I decided we would have to separate. I had grown up in what I would call a "normal" happy family and I knew things were not right now in ours. I felt the quality of all our lives was suffering and I really wanted him to get help. So I said to him in the end, "Either you get help or you leave". So he left.'

Once away from the family home, however, he did seek help. He was prescribed a course of anti-depressants and, after six weeks of separation, came back home. 'It was just as if someone different had walked through the door,' says Lorna. 'He settled down and everything was hunky dory for a couple of years.'

Until, that is, the depression took hold again. And this time, when it struck, it was worse than ever – complicated now, and exacerbated, by the fact that, unbeknown to Lorna, Tony was beginning to drink heavily, too. 'He would stand at the door,' says Lorna, 'and look at us so strangely.' It was a terrifying experience to be confronted by a man who looked like the husband she loved but who behaved like a sinister stranger. At a loss for words Lorna says simply, 'He looked mad. And Amy [then aged nine] was too scared to be with him on her own.'

In an effort to make things at least tolerable Lorna tried, with varying degrees of success, to separate the man from the illness. To say to herself and to her two frightened children that there was a reason for this strange behaviour. Dad was ill. But the rational barrier was no protection against the emotional damage. Things were clearly moving towards a crisis. In September 1992 Tony left home again. He was never to return.

Three years after his death the family is probably through the worst but the nagging doubts persist. The 'what-ifs' and the 'if-onlys'. 'If only we'd told him we loved him more,' says Lorna, not fully convinced that it would have had any effect. What if he had stayed at home? Would things have been any better then? Lorna sadly thinks not. 'I was fighting against the illness and the person who was bringing that illness into the home. If he had stayed we would both have been brought down by it. The fact is he needed help. More help than I could have given him at home. He pushed away everyone who wanted to help him. He refused all offers of rooms in friends' houses to tide him over until things got better. He spurned everyone. In the end we had to separate – to preserve the family.'

Christmas of 1992 is etched on their minds as a 'horrendous' event. All the time that Lorna and the children spent with Lorna's parents was overshadowed by the knowledge that Tony was alone in a strange room, refusing to take up any of the invitations from friends, and prey to dark and threatening thoughts. 'At one time we even got a chain for the door,' she says. 'He was so frightening.' Indeed in a scene reminiscent of the Jack Nicholson film, *The Shining* (albeit minus the axe!), Tony locked Lorna in the bathroom refusing to let her out until she had come to *her* senses.

The stage was by now set for the final act of a destructive and pitiful tragedy which was to leave no one untouched. Doubtless, like so many suicides before him, Tony had wanted to end it all. Had he but known it, he had ended nothing. With his death the real pain was about to begin. For Lorna there is the agony of knowing she was the last person to see him alive and of feeling that she should have done more to prevent him from taking his life. On the night of his death she had arranged for a baby-sitter to look after Alec and Amy while she got a break from the pressure, and went out for a quiet drink with friends.

Half-way through the evening Tony arrived unexpectedly with a look on his face that Lorna will never forget. 'He looked as though he was going to kill me. And I honestly think he would have.' Lorna's friends saw a dreadful look in his eye that told them all he was capable of something terrible. And so it was to prove.

This was all the harder for Lorna since she still loved him; loved Tony, that is, not the stranger he had become. 'I met him when I was 16 and I always assumed we were going to be together. I always felt he was going to be part of my life. I had tried everything to keep us together. We even went to family mediation which was presided over by a retired judge. Tony went along and said nothing but kept his arms folded and his face set in a scowl throughout it all. At the end the judge said,

"If I were you I would go and see a solicitor". I was glad he had said that in a way because at least it meant that someone else was aware of what I was going through and how difficult it was living with Tony.'

By the time of the last meeting, Lorna had very reluctantly embarked on the preliminary stage of the legal process of separation – a fact which Tony now took very badly. During a very public row in the streets he accused her falsely of always being out of the house and on the look-out for a new man. Nothing could have been further from the truth. She was hoping that the legal moves (which had been forced on her by necessity) would succeed in persuading him to seek help as he had before. Basically she wanted him to be himself again and for life to go on as normal.

In the state Tony was in that hope was as simple as it was impossible. Depression had driven him to a point where all personal appeals were useless. No light could now penetrate his darkness. The two of them faced each other in the street and, by now at the limit of her own endurance, Lorna heard herself, uncharacteristically, screaming, 'F . . . off. I don't care what you do'. And that was the last thing she said to him. As she watched him drive away she was physically sick with distress and was taken home to spend a fitful night before waking up to go to work 'as normal'.

Lorna went out, not surprisingly, in a state of great anxiety and with the baleful premonition that her husband was already dead. 'Don't ask me how I knew,' she says, 'I just did.' In the afternoon she returned home to take the dog for a walk and met several of the neighbours who told her the police were looking for her. She had no need to be told why.

What she remembers now is sitting in the kitchen with a friend as the policeman walked in and gave her the details of the suicide – Tony had driven off to a lonely spot, attached a hose to the exhaust, and gassed himself in his car. She greeted the news without any trace of surprise and with a numbness she thinks must have shocked the policeman. 'I'm sure he must have thought "this woman's husband has killed himself and she can't even cry". But the fact is I just knew. I suppose when you've lived with someone for so long you just get these vibes.'

Numbness, however, soon gave way to raw pain which swept over the entire family and left no one unharmed. Anger and sadness, regret and guilt combined to form a deep depression that settled on each individual member of the family. Lorna, who at the age of 33 was plunged into depression for the first time in her life, says the worst of it was to watch young Alec lying listlessly on his bed saying that it might be his destiny to commit suicide just as his father had done. To which her only answer was, 'I don't think you would do it because I know you wouldn't want to hurt anyone as much as your dad hurt us'.

'You can deal with your own hurt,' she says, 'but what I find hard to accept is the hurt he inflicted on other people, on his sister, on my parents (my mum loved Tony like another son, she really loved him) and, most of all, on his own children.'

Following the death family, friends, doctors, psychiatrists, teachers and many others moved swiftly to limit the emotional damage. The children were counselled by wise and understanding people who nursed them through the trauma. But even three years after the shocking event evidence of the trauma remains.

True, the family is closer for the experience and Lorna believes it has made them stronger and more compassionate individuals. But look at Alec's occasionally distant expression, hear him softly sigh and it is clear that great pain has been visited on the family. Even now Alec finds it hard to accept that he was not able to cry immediately the news was broken to him. Particularly hard to bear is the fact that before he knew his father had died he himself was having a happy time with friends. When the facts were told to him he felt doubly distressed; not only because he had not been there with his father to talk him out of it, but also that he had actually *been enjoying himself* while his father lay dead in the car.

The family will survive. Of that Lorna is convinced. But they have all been dreadfully hurt. And there may be more hurt yet to come for the ripples, fainter now but just as real, may not yet have finished their inevitable journey across the pond to break noiselessly on a distant shore.

'Immediately after his death,' says Lorna, 'I went through all the emotions including, bizarrely enough, sheer rage that he had robbed me of the right to do what he had done.' In other words, although she had never given suicide a second (or even a first) thought hitherto, she now felt irrational anger that he had taken from her the 'soft option' of ending her own life. 'I was now condemned to having to carry on, no matter what.'

What also changed was Lorna's attitude to the world. It felt like a sad and dangerous place to be. 'I didn't have newspapers for a year,' she says, 'because they seemed to be full of stories of suicide all the time. They seemed to stare out of the pages at me.'

Then there is the great and undeserved sense of shame. 'People don't know the whole story. They just think he killed himself because we were horrible to him' – a feeling not helped by the inquest where the distinct impression was given that marital separation had been the root cause of his death rather than the depression which had provoked the separation in the first place. 'What hurts,' she says, 'is that people don't know our story.'

Then there is the physical pain. In the days, weeks and months afterwards the whole family *felt* awful – as if someone had punched them in the chest or the stomach. 'I remember when I did break,' says Lorna, 'and I cried and cried and screamed. From being unable to cry in front of the policeman I just became distraught and broke down.' The doctor came round and gave her a sedative and the next thing she remembers is waking up surrounded by the entire collection of Amy's soft toys which a confused and vulnerable daughter had lovingly arranged around her mother's bed.

Then came the grief and the bouts of irrational rage. Irrational because one minute she would be shouting, 'I hope you can see us all, Tony. I hope you can see how you've hurt us all' and at the next she would be saying, 'If only you were here to see how we've coped since you left us in this mess. You would be so proud of us.'

They are all expressions of a love that Tony tragically could only turn his back on. Or rather, that other person turned his back on, that odd and distant stranger who looked like Tony but who wasn't. The legacy that stranger left, however, is real enough. 'I think I've had worse depressions than Tony,' says

Lorna. 'I remember one night I did wonder whether I should take the kids, cuddle up with both of them in the car, and do what he did just so we could be with him. A very dangerous thought. Because the children were so upset, they would probably have gone along with it and done anything just to be with their dad.'

Thankfully she resisted the sly pull of self-indulgence and lived on, the whole family all the stronger for having endured the worst of traumas. 'I think we've gone through the ultimate pain. Nothing can top that,' she says with understated but justifiable pride.

The sheer effort to survive has been huge; that much Lorna knows from her own depression. But she knows equally that she has been helped to cope by others who have listened patiently while she poured her heart out to them. The tragedy in Tony's case was that he seemed incapable of expressing his feelings. 'He was brought up to believe it was not what you did if you were a man,' she says. 'He always thought that saying you couldn't cope was a sign of weakness. So he continually put on this front. As far as most people knew he was fine. But behind the mask he wasn't. If he could have talked to someone like The Samaritans, that might have done some good. But he found it impossible to say, 'Help!'

The family, under Lorna's shrewd guidance, are not making the same mistake. They are talking about their feelings, sharing their upset, and refusing to hide any aspect of their painful experiences. Lorna encourages the children to talk about their father in the most natural of ways. They visit the crematorium, trawl through the family photograph album, and have sat round the fire writing him letters which they have then placed quietly in the flames.

Moving house was another stage in the process of healing. Lorna had first considered all manner of eccentric schemes, the most outlandish of which was to emigrate to Australia. But she wisely told herself to do nothing for a year on the grounds that premature decisions would probably turn out to be disastrous ones which she would live to regret. At one time she thought of moving to Cambridge to be nearer her parents but the child psychologist said it would be inadvisable to take Alec from his school. So she waited patiently, listening to advice and getting by from day to day.

When they did finally move house – from one side of town to the other – they took with them all their happy memories and contrived to leave behind what reminded them of the bad times. Tony's car was sent to a scrap yard and crushed into a cube of metal: 'I just couldn't bear the thought that I might see it one day in town'.

As for Tony, he is gone but not forgotten. Photographs and mementoes have survived the move from one house to another and life goes on. But not as it did. When Tony took his own life he took something of that old life with him; something that could never be replaced. 'Depression is a terrible thing,' says Lorna philosophically. 'And so is suicide. If only you could get through to them and say, "Think of all the people you'll leave behind". I think of Malcolm, Tony's best friend and mine, and Alec's godfather. We call him an honorary uncle because he's better than an ordinary one. Malcolm was an alcoholic but he managed to stay dry for a long time. Then six months after Tony's death he hit the bottle again and I thought, "Tony, you bastard. You let your friend down. You didn't help him by doing this." I felt so cross.'

But her anger is overshadowed by infinite tenderness and her thoughts on her husband's last moments alone in a fume-filled car are testimony to her deep love for him. 'I sit there and wonder what was going through his mind,' she says. 'How long did he have to wait? Did he just fall to sleep? Sometimes I hope he hated me at that moment. I sometimes want to believe that he hated me so much in his last moments that he decided to inflict the ultimate hurt. Because it's preferable to imagine that than to think that he lay there alone feeling so sad and thinking nobody in the world loved him. That, to me, is much worse. Because we did love him. We always will. And he didn't know what he left behind.'

There is, however, an ambivalent postscript to the story. Tony had sought help for his depression before and had been treated very successfully with anti-depressants. At the inquest it emerged that he had seen his doctor some months before his suicide and been prescribed some tablets. What is still not known is whether he had the prescription made up – let alone whether he took any medication. On balance Lorna thinks it likely that he did not.

And this is where she differed from her husband. While he may have had an inbuilt resistance to taking drugs (perhaps through a mistaken belief that it was a sign of weakness not to be able to cope) she, in her depression following his death, did as she was advised. She took the medication as it was prescribed (on one occasion provoking the pharmacist to wonder aloud how she was managing to stand up straight with so many drugs inside her!) and she underwent the talking therapies as they were offered. And as she herself puts it: 'The family's still here. We've survived.'

But, oh, how they miss Tony.

* * *

The Samaritans have a theory. Most people, they say, do not want *to die*. Rather they want *not to live*. There is a difference.

Simon Armson, the organisation's Chief Executive, expresses it as follows: 'A lot of people who talk to us describe a mental state where they simply can't conceive of life continuing the way it is. And often the way that's articulated is along the lines of "I just want to go to bed. I want to go to sleep and I want to wake up when it's better" or "I don't want to wake up until it's better", or "unless it's better". Which is a very different thing from saying, "I want to kill myself". Wanting to end your life is a very active, aggressive idea which requires energy. It's not very often that people in the very depths of a major clinical depression will have the energy to kill themselves.'

'That energy comes, paradoxically, when they begin to recover. When they are beginning to see the light at the end of the tunnel.' This is the danger zone. For it is at this point, when they catch a glimmer of the light, only to see it eclipsed once again in their general fluctuation of mood, that they fall back into the trough which is hated as much as it is feared. 'And it's at that stage,' says Simon Armson, 'when the energy's beginning to return, when the sap is beginning to rise again that they will often have the emotional means by which to kill themselves.'

It is one thing to sit it out through an emotional winter, to be marooned in the dark loneliness of a chronic depressive illness. God knows, that is bad enough. But then to have the curtain drawn back for just long enough to see a tantalising chink of spring sunshine which may be blotted out as capriciously as it first appeared is too much for many to take.

So it is at the very moment when bleak winter is giving way to an uncertain spring that some individuals will take their lives. Far from being encouraged by the lure of health they are simply reminded of the depth of their sickness and find it impossible to have to go through all that again. The promise of an emotional springtime is seen as no more than a heartless taunt, proof that they are right to think they have no role to play in such an uncaring world. Was this what T. S. Eliot meant when he described April as 'the cruellest month'?

What The Samaritans are keen to do, if it is at all possible, is to reach people before they get to the point at which they have decided that life cannot continue. Although the phrase is difficult to define accurately, they are anxious to reach people in the 'pre-suicidal state', that is to say before the stage at which they are either engaged in or planning their self-destruction.

That state is anything up to and including 'one stop short of the end of the line'. Recognising such a state, however, is not easy – even for trained volunteers. Says Simon Armson, 'The people who talk with us are in all sorts of states. Some are incoherent with distress. Others are very logical, very cogent, very self-effacing. They will say, "I'm very sorry to bother you. I'm not about to jump out of the window but I've got some things that are troubling me." And we say, "OK let's talk about them." And as we talk it becomes very clear that they are very deeply troubled. So much so that if they hadn't taken the step to reach out for emotional support at that point then they may be heading for that stage at which they simply cannot go on coping any longer.'

As part of their Defeat Depression Campaign, the Royal Colleges of Psychiatrists and of GPs have drawn up a broad outline of danger signals for doctors to take note of if they fear individuals are at risk of suicide. But even the professionals are keen to stress that suicide is unpredictable and that suicidal thoughts may be present at any stage of a depressive illness.

Members of the Suicide Bereavement Support Group have their own list of signs which, taken singly or together, might indicate acute suicidal intent. These are:

- That the person is withdrawn and unable to relate to the world outside, at which point they suggest medical aid should be sought.
- That he or she has a family history of suicide.
- That there have been earlier suicide attempts.
- That there is a definite idea present of HOW the suicide might be performed, accompanied, also, by a tidying up of affairs.
- There is acute anxiety present.
- There is a dependence on drugs or alcohol.
- Individuals display a painful physical illness or show signs of chronic sleep disturbance.
- Individuals feel a sense of uselessness and worthlessness. And, in the elderly, an unwillingness to accept retirement.
- There are feelings of loneliness, isolation, or uprooting.
- The person has no philosophy of life; for example, a comforting type of religious faith.
- There are severe financial worries.

Clearly, taken by themselves, none of these categories is a guarantee that suicide is a danger but the presence of some of them within a personality that is already in a depressed state should raise the alarm. In these circumstances it would be wise to seek advice from health professionals. And, as always, the first port of call should be the GP's surgery.

The Samaritans, founded in 1953 to provide confidential emotional support to people in crisis, has developed its own unique strategy over the years. 'The first and most important thing,' says Simon Armson, 'is that we accept and we absorb. So what we are keen to do when people ring us up, come and see us, write to us or e-mail us is to accept them as human beings in a state of emotional need.' On the face of it, this is not much for a nationally and internationally acclaimed crisis service to offer. But its deceptively simple philosophy has been of value to millions.

'We don't judge, we don't diagnose, we don't prescribe,' says Simon Armson. 'We simply accept. It might take a long time. It might take many contacts. But we help them to unburden themselves of the negative feelings that, all too often, will have been building up for a long time. So these feelings are brought out into the open in a process of "active listening" which is in itself therapeutic.'

In other words, The Samaritans believe that the mere act of talking and knowing you are being heard is of practical emotional help. Callers may be lucid or confused, angry or complacent; they may ramble on for hours or lapse into long silence. For those who ramble on there will be no interruptions, for those who are lost for words there will be no embarrassed attempt to keep the conversation going. The Samaritan will listen – as much to your silence as to your stream of consciousness. And for many that act of communication, that rare moment of having their innermost anxieties taken seriously may be the first stage in the relief of a depression. There may be many more stages needed before the depression lifts (and The Samaritans would not claim to be able to lift it unaided) but the realisation that someone need not be alone in his or her distress is a significant first step.

The approach differs completely from that adopted by doctors and counsellors; it is intended not to replace it but to complement it. Other services prescribe and advise – something which can be of great value at certain stages of depressive illness. The Samaritans do neither of these things. Says Simon Armson, 'We have to be very careful about telling people what they should be feeling or what they should be doing with their feelings because the links that enable someone to remain in contact with us during a period of crisis are very tenuous.'

Doing anything that will snap the slender thread of contact is resisted. As a result they stop short of saying, 'This is what you should be doing. You're obviously depressed because of . . . so why don't you consider . . .' The approach makes sense for two reasons. Individuals in crisis are extraordinarily vulnerable and can be immensely suggestible. To suggest a course of action 'blind' with no prior knowledge of an individual's condition or medical history would be as dangerous as it would be irresponsible. Objectively speaking, for example, psychiatric help may be appropriate for some callers but for a Samaritan *to suggest it* would not. The Samaritan might explore possible options with callers by asking *them* how they see the problem and *together* they might arrive at a strategy. But the Samaritan is not there to advise or solve.

The second reason for this approach, as Simon Armson explains, is straightforward. 'We have to be very careful to recognise where our own limitations of competence lie. We are not and never pretend to be clinically competent to engage in discussions about the nature of depressive illness so we have to be very careful to resist entering into a sort of diagnostic and thus a subsequently prescriptive process.'

Let's return to the notional example of the would-be suicide who might, objectively speaking, benefit from psychiatric treatment. What if that person had had bad experiences with such treatment before and if his perception both of psychiatry in general and of psychiatrists in particular were negative? The well-meaning but arguably reckless suggestion that he make an immediate appointment with the very professional who had frightened him off in the first place might persuade the caller that there was some kind of conspiracy going on and that the listener, far from being on neutral ground, was part of it.

Once he puts down the receiver, unlikely to pick it up again for some time, if at all, he may well reason that if even his last resort has gone bad on him what hope is there left? And the fear is that there are now no more stops before the end of the line. As Simon Armson puts it, 'It's important not to run the risk of inadvertently cutting yourself off by appearing, in their eyes, to align yourself with something that they may have already rejected.'

What, though, of those occasions when a caller picks up the phone and threatens suicide there and then? The pills are on the table, the hose is in the car, the shotgun is loaded and ready – the stage is set. Do Samaritans not then have the duty to say, 'Don't do it!'?

The dilemma is not unfamiliar to Simon Armson: 'It's one of the most horrendous things that the Samaritan is faced with. But it does happen. The first thing is that *you* try to stay calm. You will be feeling anxious, frightened and inadequate as the person entrusted, at that moment, with someone else's life. So, first, you have got to remain in control of your own feelings. Then it's really a matter of talking and listening. Of enabling and supporting; of helping a caller look at other options. To say "you mustn't do that because I say so" is meaningless. But to say "you are in control and ultimately no one but you will decide what you do with your life" is to take their intentions seriously and personally.'

While The Samaritans stop short of saying, 'Don't do it!' they strive, through talking and listening, to defer the ultimate step. If they can buy time during which the crisis may pass then they can judge their work a success. The precious moments spent in conversation may move the caller imperceptibly forward in his or her life's course – to a point where that tiny shift in perspective makes the world look wholly different. 'No one is going to take your freedom and responsibility away from you,' the Samaritan might say. 'I can't take it from you and I don't want to. But let's explore together what it is that's brought you to the point where you have placed a loaded gun on the table in front of you. If that is your chosen escape route then I'm not going to block it for you. But can you trust me for long enough to talk through the things that have brought you to this conclusion?'

Gradually and slowly the caller may alight on solutions hitherto not considered or considered and rejected. And if that caller can say, 'Well, yes, that's possible' then a hurdle may be cleared. And with one more hurdle cleared the race looks quite different than it once did.

Sometimes, in more pressing circumstances, the race looks lost before it is over. The caller will ring to say that he or she has already swallowed the tablets or that the call is being made on a mobile phone from the front seat of a car in a sealed garage with the engine running. The same befriending principle applies – though time will be on no one's side. The Samaritan will listen first, gently encouraging the caller, if he or she so wishes, to talk about how things have reached such a point and why the person feels the need to spend what may be the last few minutes of a life with a complete stranger on the telephone. At some point the caller may express regret and ask for help. Then and only then, when specifically asked to intervene, will the Samaritan call an ambulance.

While it may seem an ambivalent philosophy at best and a heartless one at worst, the Samaritan principle is actually very positive. For a start it is practical and realistic in that there is no point offering advice if the caller does not want it in the first place (and being pushy merely increases the chances of the receiver being replaced – which is in no one's interest). What The Samaritans can do (unlike all but the most intimate and trusting of conversations) is to engage with the caller on his or her own terms. So, as The Samaritans' Director of Training, Joan Guénault, explains, 'If someone hints at suicidal thoughts, whereas the normal inclination in everyday life is to walk away from that and to start talking about the weather or something "safe", what we train ourselves to do is to move into that pain, not to walk away from it and then we help the person to explore why it is they're feeling that way.'

But more than that, The Samaritans' philosophy is one which asserts that people are in control of their own destiny. And that the responsibility to dispose of life's most precious gift – life itself – lies with the individual alone. Says Simon Armson, 'We can't take that responsibility from them. Nor can we take that opportunity and that right. But what we can do is give them the time and the space, the confidence and the trust to be able to look at things in a broader perspective. And the fact that they have taken the step to contact us and that they are talking to us means that there may now be a way forward rather than a way out.'

Time and again The Samaritans have heard an infinitely sorrowful refrain, 'I don't want to die. But I don't want to live like this.' Behind that simple 'like this' lies an endless series of uniquely painful events. Of these, of course, bereavement is one of the hardest to bear. But the end of a relationship, a divorce or an unhappy love affair, a financial crisis, or a terminal illness are all sufficient, in the right circumstances, to tip people into a depression which may temporarily unsettle the proper balance of their mind. And even the strongest prohibitions will have little effect on a personality set on self-destruction.

Suicide was decriminalised in the UK in 1961 and with that went the notion that to kill oneself was an offence to civil society. But while the legal taboo was relaxed the religious taboo is strangely persistent. For many Christians, for example, particularly for Catholics, it is considered a sin – though the Church is now more inclined to show sympathy and compassion to those who have actually gone ahead and taken their own lives than it once did in the days when suicides were refused burial in hallowed ground.

Despite existential arguments that it is the ultimate exercise of one's free will there is a strong belief, in Christian circles, that to do such harm against oneself is wrong. Few nowadays would argue with the same force as G. K. Chesterton did against suicide in his book *Orthodoxy* but there is a residual attachment to the gist of his conviction which it is worth quoting at length:

> ❛Not only is suicide a sin, it is the sin. It is the ultimate and absolute evil, the refusal to take the oath of loyalty to life. The man who kills a man kills a man. The man who kills himself kills all men; as far as he is concerned he wipes out the world. His act is worse (symbolically considered) than any rape or dynamite outrage. For it destroys all buildings; it insults all women. The thief is satisfied with diamonds; the suicide is not: that is his crime. He cannot be bribed, even by the blazing stones of the Celestial City. The thief compliments the things he steals, if not the owner of them. But the suicide insults everything on earth by not stealing it. He defiles every flower by refusing to live for its sake. There is not a tiny creature in the cosmos at whom his death is not a sneer. When a man hangs himself on a tree, the leaves might fall off in anger and the birds fly away in fury: for each has received a personal affront . . . There is meaning in burying the suicide apart. The man's crime is different from other crimes – for it makes even crimes impossible. ❜

This is all very well for as long as one is within reach of rational argument (or, as in this case, reasoned censure). The problem with deep depression is that it encloses the sufferer in a self-contained and private world beyond the reach of all such appeals. In such a state suicide can be triggered by the most minor of extra pressures.

What The Samaritans can do is to accept the telephone call, brief as it may be, as a privilege bestowed on them by a stranger in crisis. Then they can use it as a breathing space between a stated intention and an unresolved future. As the two talk privately together the situation is changing all the time, deferring with each passing minute, the ultimate step. To recast the cliché 'where there's life there's hope' (a meaningless platitude to the would-be suicide and one which flatly contradicts his or her personal experience) – to recast it into a form which may be more acceptable 'where there's talk there's life'.

Lest it be thought that The Samaritans are dangerously equivocal about suicide let it be said that they are not. They do not welcome violent death. They want to care for and support the man or woman who feels impelled to take his or her own life. But they do so not by saying, 'Do not kill yourself. Suicide is wrong.' Rather they say, 'Let us keep talking, my friend. And between us we may discover that life is worth living.' The mere fact that a caller has picked up the phone opens the door on the most fragile of opportunities, and lets in the most tenuous ray of light into a room full of darkness.

* * *

The well of human misery is apparently bottomless. And unhappiness comes tailor-made to suit every individual. That said, trends are clearly visible and worrying patterns are beginning to emerge that anxiety and depression are not completely random. For example, according to statistics published by The Samaritans, who have themselves drawn on data from the Office of Population, Censuses and Surveys, the number of men dying by suicide outnumbers women by four to one. This compares to two to one in 1982.

There may be underlying reasons for this pattern but identifying them with any degree of precision is notoriously difficult. Hypotheses, however, have been suggested. Drink and drug abuse, for example, are far more common in men than they are in women. The problem here, of course, is deciding whether the alcoholism or the drug addiction is a cause or symptom of the primary depression. Either way, abuse of such substances is known to be a contributory factor in the incidence of suicide. Men seem to fare worse than women in the absence of a close partner. So single, divorced, and widowed men are in a higher-risk group with suicide rates (among such men over the age of 24) three times greater than those of married men.

Studies have suggested that morale at work is at an all-time low as the recession sends a chill of fear and anxiety throughout the workforce. Contracts are getting shorter, hours are getting longer, and the pressure to be seen to be performing well in an increasingly competitive environment is now commonplace. Older men feel threatened by new recruits and have found it difficult to adapt to the inescapable fact that jobs for life belong to a vanished age. Those who are in work are working harder than ever, pushing up their stress levels and running the risk of extra anxiety caused by a fragmented family life.

Low morale at work, however, is often as nothing when compared with the stress of unemployment and the depression such an event engenders. With the loss of a job come feelings of failure and humiliation, diminished self-esteem and worthlessness. Loss of status chips away at a person's identity which very often is defined by what that person does. Redundancy and long-term unemployment frequently lead to a sense of pointlessness which in turn can put great strain on personal relationships. And clearly the financial blow dealt either to a single man or to his family can be devastating. In addition it has been suggested that men are much more likely to repress their emotions. Bottling up an emotion seems much more prevalent in men than in women who have traditionally not been afraid to display emotions (particularly of sadness and grief) in public.

Such pressures may suggest broadly why men are under greater pressure than before but no one has explained adequately why vets and dentists should top the suicide table. Nor has it been convincingly explained why there has been such a dramatic rise in suicide rates among farmers and agricultural workers. Isolation and easier access to poisons and firearms may be reasons but there must be more complex factors at play than these alone.

There is a particular sense of concern for the growing number of prisoners who take their own lives. To be in a prison within a prison is surely a double punishment the penal system did not intend or, to be fair, could not have foreseen. But especially worrying is the rise in suicide among young men under 25. In 1982, seven young men in every 100,000 killed themselves. Since then the figure has risen to 12 in every 100,000 – an increase of 71 per cent. This group now has a higher suicide rate than that of the overall population in the UK – currently 10 per 100,000. Again, it is dangerous to offer simple explanations as to why this might be – although unemployment, family breakdown, abuse and attendant homelessness are clearly contributory factors.

What we are left with in the face of uncomfortable statistics such as these is an abiding sense of loss and waste – lost hopes and youthful promise, wasted talents and years that could have been infused with happiness. That is not, of course, how the suicide and the chronic depressive see things. They are more inclined to side with one of Samuel Beckett's characters who ventures to suggest that woman gives birth astride the grave and after a brief flash of light all is darkness once again.

But surely, we reason, there is more to life than that. Children, love, music, art, iced water on a baking day, friends, laughter, food, a faithful pet, a good book, or a room with a view . . . Even Beckett, in his classic *Waiting for Godot,* locks his characters in a bleak landscape that yet admits of hope. They may wait eternally for a redeemer who never shows – or, at least, who hasn't shown so far – but still they wait. They are heroes for our uncertain times, heroes whose courage and humour can still induce us to go on.

For another modern writer, Albert Camus, the question of suicide was the only serious philosophical problem. *The Myth of Sisyphus* reinterprets the Greek legend of Sisyphus, who was condemned to roll a boulder to the top of a hill only to see it roll down again before it reaches its destination. In the end Camus concludes that Sisyphus was a happy man. Life, he seemed to be saying among many other philosophical speculations, is hard. But life is all we can be sure we have.

Life is very hard. But it can, in the company of another beating heart, be endured. Conveying that to a would-be suicide, or to someone locked in the peculiar hell of clinical depression is the challenge to us all. The following suggestions (in some cases, given by people who have themselves contemplated suicide, in others, by people whose friends or relatives have taken the ultimate step) may be useful at the time of maximum crisis.

If you are alone and have decided to kill yourself, no one can stop you. In those circumstances:

- Are you able to phone someone? If you are, can you consider making the effort to call. At least you will no longer be alone – though you may still be determined to kill yourself.
- If you have no family or friends, would you consider a call to The Samaritans? You may still be suicidal but at least your loneliness can be shared.
- You know what you are getting out of. But can you be sure what you are getting into? Death – Hamlet's 'undiscover'd country from whose bourn no traveller returns' – may not be the end but the beginning.
- Can you be certain you will die a painless death? What if the tablets do not kill you immediately but damage your liver irreparably so that you die in hospital a week later?
- If you are about to leap, can you be sure you will have no second thoughts before you hit the ground or the water?
- What if you succeed only in injuring yourself permanently?
- Your destiny is in your hands. If you are about to run under a train, the driver will think that your destiny was in his hands. Are you prepared to leave the consequences of your actions with someone else?
- If you are troubled by any one of the last five questions, can you pause for a moment? Do you have the strength to defer your decision?

- If you are actively on the brink of taking your life, you have reached the point of maximum pain it is possible for a human being to endure. If you succeed in killing yourself no one will know how much you have suffered. Your note was written earlier and will be invalid at the point of death. Can you find the energy to tell someone how bad it is?
- If you are about to take your life, life will now have become as bad as it can possibly be. By definition it cannot get worse. Are you able, intellectually at least, to hold on to that concept?
- If you die without family or friends, a number of people will still be affected somehow by your death. Do you have the strength or the inclination to add them up?
- If you die leaving family behind, how do you feel about the possibility that your despair may be transferred to them?
- If you think your death will serve them all right, are you able to see that your anger may be a positive reason for holding on to life?
- Tears will be shed by someone at your funeral. Can you find the strength or the will to find out who they are?
- If you die, someone somewhere will say, 'I had no idea s/he felt like that?' Do you have the strength to tell them, face to face or on the phone?
- No one will be better off without you.

* * *

'No man is an island.' However tenuous it may feel at times, we are all connected to the mainland. Perhaps the only thing we can do is to repeat it (or reinterpret it) often and compassionately enough to people when they are well so that they might just manage to believe it when they are not. It is not easy and there are no guarantees of success but perhaps, as T. S. Eliot wrote, 'for us there is only the trying'. Perhaps all we can do is to persuade them of our love and support and try to convince them that with their death we, their loved ones on the mainland, are diminished, too.

* * *

Jo is 50, a level-headed Hampshire woman living with her husband and two daughters in a village near Winchester, in a
beamed cottage that could feature on any picture postcard. No
one, least of all Jo herself, would have expected this model of
placid family life to be disrupted by sudden, unnatural death.
But disrupted it was when first her mother then her father took
their own lives in the depth of their own depressions.

'No one ever knows why people take their own lives,' she
says five years after the loss of her mother and three years after
the death of her father, 'but I think my mother killed herself
because she was in a lot of pain and because she saw no way out
of her depression.' She had just moved house, too, and because
of her restricted mobility could not get out to meet people as
often as she would have liked. Gradually she became isolated
and as her isolation grew so, too, did the feelings of hopeless-
ness.

At the time Jo was herself a Samaritan and had recognised
signs that might indicate suicidal intent – alienation, depression,
the tendency to push people away from herself, and a couple of
previous attempts on her life. Jo is honest enough with herself
and others to admit that the two roles, one as a Samaritan, the
second as loving daughter, were in conflict, provoking a tension
that she did not ultimately resolve.

It is worth reminding ourselves, however, that Samaritans are
human, too, and might be wrong-footed by emotional events in
the midst of their own families. And that, yes, they might find
themselves inadvertently breaking the rules with people closer
to home. 'The Samaritan bit of me was trying to do what I could
to help,' she says, 'and the other bit of me was saying, "Help! I
can't handle this".'

Her mother, then aged 76, had always been a closed person
but when the shutters came down she retreated into herself
completely and communication became impossible. Even so,
knowing all the danger signals did not prepare her for the shock
of picking up the telephone one morning and hearing her father
telling her that her mother was dead.

He had discovered the body when he walked into her bedroom that morning. Although she looked peaceful enough by

the time Jo arrived, one can only imagine the shock her father felt as he opened the door to be confronted by the body of his wife, her head covered in two plastic bags which she had tied round her throat with a cord. News of this gruesome discovery provoked shock and, Jo now admits, a tinge of horror at the disturbing nature of the death. She raced round to the house in something like hysteria to be met by the doctor, called to certify that she was indeed dead; by the police, who were now signalling to the neighbourhood, in an unavoidably public way, that something dreadful had happened; and by the undertaker, who confirmed the neighbours' darkest suspicions.

Numbness took the place of shock for some six months after the death. This was to be succeeded by an enormous amount of anger. 'I was livid,' she now recalls. 'The anger wasn't directed *at* anyone (I probably was angry at her but I couldn't admit it). I was just angry.' Her two daughters remember vividly how they felt and make no attempt to disguise it now. 'I was furious she had left Grandpa,' says Sarah, 24 and the elder of the two, now at university. The girls had not been told of their grandmother's first suicide attempt but when she had attempted it a second time Jo thought it right to keep nothing from her daughters and to tell them the details of both events.

Even this did not prepare Sarah for the shock of an actual death. 'In some ways I felt relieved because I felt she was probably happier dead. I wasn't getting on with her very well at the time and I knew she was miserable but I was furious because it left Grandpa on his own with no one to look after him. And looking after her had been his whole life. This just left him with a void.'

Then came the self-recriminations. Sarah felt bad about not visiting her as often as she now felt she ought to have done. Why hadn't she gone to see her more – after all, she only lived down the road? Why had she been too busy doing other things? Why hadn't she made more of an effort? And so on and so on. The daughters remember that their grandmother had been very unhappy over a number of years before her death. They remember her, too, as someone who seemed to have been ill for as long as they had known her – constantly in and out of hospitals. The depression seemed merely part of that general pattern of ill health.

Jo's husband, Ivor, is able to stand back a little from the kind of emotional turmoil which engulfed Jo herself. 'I felt that she seemed determined to do it at some stage,' he says. 'She had made two attempts already and it somehow seemed inevitable that she would do it again and succeed. In a funny sort of a way it was almost a relief that it had finally occurred. But I was angry, too, because now we had to deal with the mess she'd left behind.'

Ivor was left having to cope not only with Jo's sadness but also with the residual guilt she was unjustifiably feeling. Several years earlier her parents had uprooted themselves from London in order to be nearer them and the grandchildren. In the process they had left behind all their friends and acquaintances whom they had built up over time. Moving into the provinces, therefore, had had an isolating effect which Ivor believes Jo may have felt vaguely guilty about. Sudden death did nothing to ease that feeling. Ivor, who had never been particularly close to his mother-in-law, felt annoyed that her suicide had now put undeserved emotional pressure on Jo, and had left his father-in-law virtually abandoned. 'It was an easy way out for her,' he says, 'but it left him with all the problems. Problems which he had spent all his life trying to share with her.'

Lucy, the younger daughter who was 15 at the time, registered only sorrow. She had been much closer to her grandmother than the others and had made a point of 'trying to be good' for her, often going round to cook her lunches and so on. 'I don't remember being angry with anyone when she died,' she says. 'But I remember being very upset.' For her the suicide was just a death, the death of someone for whom she had felt great affection. Lucy found that what was going through other people's minds at the time was, in a sense, being projected on to her. She, by contrast, had none of the conflicting emotions of guilt, anger and regret. She had simply lost a person who had been close to her. And that was that. Or almost. Because, although she feels that her grandma's suicide was an essentially neutral event, not to be judged in any moral terms ('It's a way of dying,' she says), when her friend at university talked of her own depression and of her suicidal feelings Lucy found her own reaction quite different. 'I got incredibly angry with her,' she says, 'but that's because she's my age.'

So while Lucy may have been privately appalled that her contemporary should consider ending her life prematurely, she may also have unconsciously thought that a 76-year-old woman who was depressed and ill should have the right to dispose of hers as she wished. A kind of voluntary euthanasia. That is not how the rest of the family viewed it.

Jo is aware of the terrible shadow such a death casts on a family. 'It dumps an awful lot on the people who are left behind,' she says. 'All the unfinished business will now NEVER be finished. It's a big rejection of those who are left and the feelings are very difficult to cope with. It's not like a conventional death at all. Your reactions change all the time.'

'Rejection, particularly for an only child like me, was very hard to cope with. But it was the anger I found the worst. I didn't know what it was nor where it was coming from and, until I found a creative way to deal with it, I felt I was going to explode. It was so powerful.' The 'heavy sadness' that now settled on her life was also tinged with confusion. Why had her mother done it? But this, she now frustratingly had to accept, was a conundrum that would never be resolved. Not only that but, from her work with cancer patients, Jo knew the importance of tidying up relationships before one's death. 'One of the nastiest things about it all,' she says, 'was not having been able to say goodbye.'

The love Jo felt for her mother is clear to see and, even when she speaks of her anger, the tears well up to the surface. The anger was partly on her daughters' behalf (how *could* she do that to them?) and partly on her own account (how could she do *that* to me) and then the anger was directed at her mother (*why* did you have to do it?). Yet, in a curious and confused way, she knew why her mother had done it and felt it wrong to feel angry with her. This, in turn, provoked a cold undirected fury. 'I had a very low flash point at the time,' she says, 'but, because of the work I do, I tried not to turn it towards anyone.'

But the fury was still there. 'What really incensed me,' Jo now recalls, 'was that she had in effect said that my kids weren't worth living for. And, of course, that I, her own daughter, wasn't worth living for either. That hurt.' And there was more hurt to come because, in the aftermath of the suicide, her father now retreated into himself and began to shut everyone else out of his world as her mother had done from hers.

A few days before she died she uncharacteristically invited everyone round for a drink. In retrospect Jo can see this as the classic sign which went, nonetheless, unheeded at the time. Her mother seemed to be on the mend. She had got her strength and spirits up sufficiently to entertain them all and everything seemed suddenly fine. But Jo had not forgotten that two failed suicide attempts had lowered the threshold of her fear of death. If death no longer held such terror, then dying might be preferable to this constant, corrosive bleakness. Her revitalised mood merely sharpened her resolve, 'Better death than this living hell'.

The tragedy for the family was that her mood was being misread and that her intentions could not have been guessed at. As they parted after an unexpectedly pleasant evening together for what they could not have known would be the last time, Jo and her daughters said goodbye in the expectation of seeing her soon, while their grandmother said farewell, uncertain whether she would ever see them again.

The death left Jo's father devastated. All the more hurt and rejected because the two of them had discussed taking their own lives together (unbeknown to Jo and to her horrified incomprehension). Now that she had done it without him – without even telling him that she planned to do it in the next room while he slept – he was inconsolable. 'He was quite an angry person,' says Jo, 'but with Mum's death he lost his anger.'

From being the once assertive, indeed aggressive person that Ivor remembers he became suddenly passive. From the moment he had stepped into his wife's bedroom on that indelible morning, gently loosening the tape round her neck, and pulling back the two plastic bags from her face, he was never the same again. Life lost its purpose. 'What's the point?' became his constant lament as relatives and friends vainly tried to encourage him. He lost interest in everything, lacking the energy sometimes to eat. Everything became too much trouble for him and it was all he could do to take himself off (alone) to the coast in nearby Hythe. But even his once-keen interest in boats suddenly became dulled. His granddaughters tried to get him out of the house, taking him for walks when they could, but they were aware of fighting a losing battle against his increasing apathy. Eventually he seemed to have given up altogether preferring to sit in an armchair, watch the news, and go to bed.

Sarah admits she had always got on better with her grandfather than with her grandmother so she was doubly disturbed by events. Disturbed by her suicide, of course, but disturbed, too, by the state he had now been reduced to as a result of it. 'It used to upset me that she'd just left him on his own,' she says. 'It was like a divorce but worse. With a divorce you still have a person to negotiate with. With a suicide there's nobody left to argue with.'

His natural independence hardened into isolation as he insisted on keeping everyone at arm's length. It was true that he could occasionally confide in his daughter but only to repeat how depressed he was and (troublingly) how suicidal he felt. 'He would tell me how he intended to do it,' says Jo, 'and at times would talk to me as if I were a Samaritan – which was excruciatingly difficult. Face to face with my father I did all the things we're not supposed to do on the phone! I just could not deal with it at all.'

Plunged into her own despair and depression she could not, as a daughter, bear to hear him speaking like this. So she stayed away from him until the worst of the blackness passed and she could summon the strength to help. Then she could confront him with her true feelings – though to no avail. Speaking very definitely NOT as a Samaritan she would say, 'I hate what you're doing! I can understand why you're doing it but I hate it all the same.'

Nothing she could say or do could get through to him. No protestations of love, no appeals to him to remember the grandchildren would penetrate the defences he had, wilfully or otherwise, erected against the world. In the end, however, Jo was forced to accept his decision. She was simply not strong enough to fight it. His moods were like a force of nature which seemed to affect the atmosphere of any family gathering. 'When we had him round for meals,' says Jo, 'the whole mood would go down. His depression would suck us all in no matter how hard we tried. We'd all try to be bright and chatty but one by one we'd go quiet until we were all part of this dark black cloud.'

There were clear signs that he had embarked on a course from which he would not turn back. Sarah remembers him once coming into her room and admiring a picture of a dolphin she had on her wall. He looked at it almost wistfully and told her of the time, not that long ago, when he had been briefly happy again swimming with dolphins on holiday. Then he made a cryptic remark about being with them again soon and left. It was a remark which left Jo enraged, since, in her view, it should not have been made to his granddaughter.

There was a terrible inevitability about her father's suicide, all the more painful for those near because of its unpredictability. First there had been the chronic depression and the listlessness, then there had been the threats. Then in October he made an unsuccessful attempt on his life. In following weeks he maintained that Ivor and Jo must have come round during the night and interrupted him – removing, as he had once done with his wife, the two bags he had placed over his head. But no such intervention had taken place. Instead, as Jo now believes, he was not ready to die and had removed the paraphernalia of suicide half-way through. With one attempt now made, another could not be far off. The only question was when.

Although he had not intended to cause such torment, his attitude was heartlessly cruel. Before the first attempt, for example, he had written Jo a letter saying that he would be dead by the time she read it. When she did read it, in a haze of confusion and panic, she instinctively picked up the phone to call his house, only, to her horror, to hear his voice at the end of the line like some voice from beyond the grave. She and Ivor dashed round to find him in a daze, angry with himself that all his plans had been thwarted. Ivor suspects a degree of shame and humiliation, too. 'First he and his wife had had a suicide pact. Then she had betrayed him by committing suicide alone. He had then lived for a while very, very depressed and had at last screwed up courage to go the same way and then, at the last moment . . . he couldn't even do that.'

'He wasn't someone who failed,' says Sarah. 'He used to do what he set out to do.' And according to Ivor this public failure hit him hard. As for Jo, she was so angry with him that she could not speak to him for four days, her mood compounded by sorrow and rejection which she found almost too much to bear. She tried hard to save him from himself – involving the psychiatric services, counsellors, therapists, and healers – but all with no success. His tactic, she says, was to push everyone away so that he could deliberately isolate himself. Only then could he go through with it.

The long, slow build-up to the inevitable had a two-fold effect. In one sense it allowed a kind of grieving process to get under way prematurely as they prepared themselves for what they could not prevent. But on the other hand, it made them nervous, forever wondering *when* the worst would strike. 'We got to the stage when we thought the sooner it happened the easier it was going to be,' says Ivor.

By now the family was resigned to a second suicide and, as the anniversary of Jo's mother's death approached, the atmosphere in the household was tense beyond words. The anniversary came and went leaving Jo's nerves stretched like an overstrung violin. In the illusory calm that followed Jo had forgotten the anniversary of her mother's funeral. Her father had not.

'It was a huge relief when he died,' she says. 'We got the letter that morning and rushed round to his house but couldn't find him.' Their assumption had been that he had chosen to suffocate himself in the bedroom. But they were wrong. Instead he had shut himself in the garage, 'made himself comfortable' in the car, surrounded by his library books and a cup of coffee, and gassed himself.

* * *

In the intervening three years the family has had time enough to analyse the complexity of often conflicting emotions. Ivor, for example, puts any blame – if blame indeed applies – on his mother-in-law. She started it all and set in train a sequence of events which could not have been halted. Jo puts the responsibility square on her father's shoulders, though, in his absence, she pleads mitigation. 'Suicide had been an option for him since the age of eight when he watched someone walk to their death in the sea. The person walked into the waves and shortly after a body was washed up.'

It is impossible to assess the impact of that experience on her father at so impressionable an age but ever since then, according to Jo, he had said that suicide was always something he could keep in reserve, a 'viable option' he could exercise at 60 or at 70 or whenever. 'But then Mum got ill and he was forced to look after her,' she says, 'so that gave him a reason for going on.' Either way, suicide was clearly his secret weapon in a crisis, the bag he kept permanently packed by the door, the visa he knew would take him, should the irresistible journey beckon, across an unimaginable night-time frontier.

What gave him a kind of peace of mind scares the living daylights out of those he left behind. Both granddaughters have read that families can have a genetic predisposition to depression. Both of them know that a suicide in the family can prompt another years down the line, and both are frightened that they, too, might, somehow be carrying this 'virus' within them. They get all the reassurance they could hope for from loving parents but the fear is still lodged at the back of their minds. Could it happen to them? Jo remembers one particularly traumatic period, after their grandfather's suicide, when Sarah wrote of her depression at university. Jo was beside herself with worry. *Could* it happen to them? The children think not. If only because they have seen the pain it has inflicted on others.

But there are other more down-to-earth side-effects from suicide; shame for one. 'The worst bit was wandering round Sainsbury's, not knowing anyone there from Adam, and thinking that everyone was looking at me, wondering under their breath, "What's wrong with her that both her parents topped themselves?" ' And there's stigma. 'This is one of the most difficult things for survivors,' says Jo. 'The whole notion of "committing suicide" which implies a crime is not easy. Because if it is a crime then we are somehow implicated in it. The inquest, too, is often misunderstood as some sort of trial deciding on guilt and innocence rather than a neutral inquiry into the circumstances. Then there's the police and the newspapers and all that.'

Her parents' deaths also diminished her. 'My self-esteem really took a nosedive,' says Jo. 'You've been rejected so you start to reject yourself.' In other words, at its most extreme: if someone cannot be bothered to live for your sake, why should you bother to live for yourself? Willed or not, for some, suicide can feel like a curse. And certainly their grandfather's death has left traces on the girls' lives. Exhaust fumes, for example, bring it all back again. A bus goes by and a particular mixture of gas and oil takes Sarah back to the fume-filled garage. She is in a car park and a reflected light suggests someone slumped over the wheel . . .

And this, Jo reckons, was a relatively peaceful death. Not for her father, a shotgun to the head; not for her, the discovery of a hanged man in the hallway; not for Ivor, the deliberate smile the railway suicide reserves for the train driver; not for *this* family the blood or the mutilated corpse. No. All in all, a 'dignified' death. And yet . . .

After all the suffering what is Jo's view of this desperate, ultimately incomprehensible act? 'I don't feel it was wrong. I don't feel it was right either. I couldn't do it myself – not after the pain I've been through. I couldn't inflict that kind of hurt on anybody else. And when I hear anybody talking about their own suicide I get so mad.'

* * *

Suicide is a feature of depression at its most extreme; of despair at its blackest. By the time men or women have decided to kill themselves the door leading to the outside world has shut tight. Or, as in the case of Jo's father or Lorna's husband, the door has been deliberately pulled to. Either way, the door is firmly closed, admitting neither light nor hope into a private hell.

The tragedy is that, in this condition, would-be suicides are beyond all help – and certainly reading these personal accounts (even if they could summon the motivation to do so!) would be of no value to them. It is not so much that the story of someone else's suffering doesn't matter to them; it is rather that, in the suicidal state, no other story of suffering *exists*. There is only their own.

However, there is a very good reason for including such stories in this book, because for many people, while the door may be closed, it is not necessarily locked. And the infinite patience of a sympathetic listener may be enough to ease it back a fraction so that the whole landscape of this utterly private place can be viewed afresh. True, not much will have actually changed – there will still be no immediate prospect of a job for the unemployed, there will still be no change in the housing waiting list for the bed-and-breakfast dweller, and for the loveless there will still be no return of the partner who has walked out or died. But there *will* be a subtle shift in the perspective from which the despairing will view their predicament. And for some that will provide a fragile shaft of hope.

Those faced with a would-be suicide, rather than judging 'suicide is bad', should try tentatively to say 'life is good'. It is also important to try to accept the state of mind of that despairing person who disagrees. In doing that, remember not to say 'I know how you feel'. The plain fact is that *no one* knows how you feel. More appropriate would be: 'I know you feel as you do. And that it hurts. And while I cannot necessarily persuade you *out* of your despair perhaps I can try to bring you *into* something else, a state, perhaps, or a mood in which you may feel, albeit for a fleeting moment, that other things are possible. Talk and somebody will always be there to listen.' And in that conversation life will move on a little; life will not be the same again.

It is no accident that The Samaritans have installed telephones at Beachy Head and Clifton Suspension Bridge. But their purpose is not quite so obvious as it seems. The phones are not there to say 'Don't do it!'. They are there (if an imaginary sign could be made big enough) to say something like 'You alone will decide what you have to do and you alone will act accordingly. But consider picking up the phone and *postponing* your action – if only for a moment – then do what you must'.

It is not unknown for a suicidal impulse to pass. But the suicidal act cannot be revoked. Suicide is the permanent solution to what may be a temporary problem – though the problem is no less real for all that. Talking may be an equally real way of buying an invaluable moment of extra time during which the world and you move on. Talking, please note. YOU. TALKING. Not THEM talking you OUT of anything.

Of course, once embarked on a path of self-destruction, deviation from it is hard. Deviation brings with it the taunt of weakness – and, in its wake, renewed worthlessness and more than a tinge of shame. Much better to get it over with quickly! Such is only one aspect of the ambivalence of suicide, one feature of its peculiarly self-contradictory nature. There are many more but perhaps the most poignant comes in the testimony of one survivor. He, against all the odds, survived a leap from the Golden Gate Bridge in San Francisco. Not many do. But interviewed some time after his attempt, he said that even as he was walking to the edge he was prey to one insistent thought – the voice in his own head which said, 'Stop me. Somebody, stop me.' Locked as he was into his self-destructive intention he was unable to resist its siren call. If only someone had been there, or something on hand to suggest that the process could be interrupted without shame, humiliation, or further self-reproach, who knows whether he might have paused for a moment at the bridge's edge?

The aim of this book is not to prevent anyone from taking his or her own life (though I see no contradiction in adding that I hope that it does). It is simply to say time and again that a breathing space – sometimes literally a breathing space, as you will see later – between the intention and the act will project you into a world that is not the same as it was. We do not bathe in the same stream twice. The world and you will have moved on a second, maybe two seconds, maybe three hours and no one can possibly know how it will look then. In the hourglass of that eternal moment you might, just might, see a new world in a grain of sand.

More prosaically, those who fear they might take an overdose have sometimes wrapped each individual pill beforehand in a self-sealing plastic sachet. That way, when it comes to the time, they will not be able to engineer their dispatch with a grand gesture of impetuosity. They will have to involve themselves in the tiresome business of unwrapping them all again and in that time . . . who knows?

Such thinking lies behind actual or potential public policy strategies. The change from toxic gas to natural gas in the 1960s, for example, is reckoned to have reduced the number of suicides in the home. The despairing could not act on a whim by opening the oven door. Instead they might have to take a trip to the chemist to buy some pills. And in that brief time they might just be forced to reflect and draw back from the brink.

There are some researchers who suggest that similar reductions in suicide can be achieved by introducing catalytic converters to car engines and by introducing stricter controls on exhaust emissions. The temptation to use a comparatively simple method of dispatch, it is reasoned, will thus be ruled out. Such moves may or may not be effective but they are unlikely to be of any comfort to the depressed person.

And here we return to the central problem facing the terminally depressed or suicidal. While in their lucid, comparatively lighter mood they might accept all or some of the above, in their windowless prison which is the trough of their despair they can accept none of it. It does not make sense, does not apply, does not compute. It is written in the language of the living when they, all too sentient but not alive, are condemned to inhabit the house of the dead.

Afam Ejimbe, a 26-year-old professional photographer and long-term sufferer from depression, has bitter proof of this. Two weeks after the suicide of his best friend, Steve, he decided to take his own life.

The landscape of his mood is all too familiar: 'I felt I was in a room without doors and windows. There was nothing inside it, no pictures to look at, nothing to take my attention off the depression.' With nothing further to live for, he locked himself in his basement flat in South London and prepared for the end.

What makes his experience unique is that, artistic and self-expressive by nature, he decided to capture his mental state on video and to film his frenzied activities before the moment of his death. He scoured the flat in search of a means to end his life and eventually decided on hanging. He rummaged in drawers and cupboards for wires or ropes before finally settling on a dressing-gown cord which he made into a noose and attached to an overhead pipe. He had prepared for death well, estimating his weight and the drop beforehand and calculating whether he would slowly choke at the end of the cord or be dispatched with a violent jerk before his body could fall to the ground.

Before taking his life, however, he had one last thing to do. He embarked on a manic creative period during which, in homage to his favourite painter, Michelangelo, he adorned the walls of his flat with murals and drawings. These highly accomplished frescoes are still there as a constant reminder of his suicidal state of mind, depicting faces with mad, staring eyes and fantastical torsos tensed to breaking point with anguish and pain.

In the video he made he can now see his irrational self furiously working on what he thought would be his last project. He can watch himself raving and raging as he darts frantically round the flat putting his mental condition into pictorial form. Standing outside the experience now, he can see the objectively disordered state he was in but stepping outside that experience then was impossible. He was trapped inside it and incapable of communication with the outside world.

By now the momentum driving Afam along a predictable trajectory of despair was seemingly unstoppable. 'I wanted to be in a place where there were no more questions,' he says, 'no more paintings, no more worries, no more pain.' He raised the noose and knew that 'when the loop goes round your neck you're already dead.'

He paused. In that split second he thought back to Steve, and let out one last despairing appeal to his dead friend. 'I was so angry,' he says, 'I called out to Steve and asked him whether this was really it. Whether this was really the sum total of my life.' This most fragile connection with something outside his own head was enough to open the door to his particular prison, allowing in the tiniest thread of light – but it was enough to save his life. 'Then I thought of my mum,' he says, 'and that broke it.'

The door was now opening that little bit further, letting in more precious light. Next (although all this was done in the space of a few seconds) he thought back to his primary school days and to Mrs Dougal who took him to the seaside, encouraged him to draw, and showed an interest in him while at home his father used to beat him.

Such kindness, long ago occluded by his father's daily cruelties, welled up in his mind and held out its saving hand to him. Thinking back to the times when he had known happiness, to the moments of contentment he had once known before the depressions had settled on him, he took hold of the hand and, shaking violently from head to foot, let it lead him gently off the chair to solid ground.

There was no immediate happy ending. Afam was to spend the next two days stark naked on the hall floor staring blankly up at the noose. He was not out of his depression but he was alive. Somehow the door to his darkened prison cell, from which even he felt there could be no escape, was softly pushed ajar. And it is to the possibility of such momentary intervention that The Samaritans and others hold fast – often more in hope than in expectation. The door to life may be shut but there is no way of knowing ultimately whether it is locked on the inside.

6

Facing the Future: Caring and Listening

A minority of depressed people kill themselves. Most simply endure. And one of the distinguishing features of their depression is a sense of personal isolation. That is painful enough. Being cut off from those you love is doubly hard. For everyone. When a father or a mother, a son or a daughter, a husband or a wife is depressed the rest of the family suffers from the fall-out and the atmosphere in the household is transformed. Most people are unprepared for it.

It is as if the sufferer is on one side of a thick pane of plate glass and the carer is on the other. Each can see clearly what is happening and each is equally powerless to intervene. It is this sense of impotence which often causes the greatest anxiety and stress which, in their turn, feed off themselves to generate even more tension in the family. The tragedy is that 'doing what comes naturally' is not always the most effective solution and misjudging the approach to take (albeit with the best intentions) can sometimes make things worse.

In what follows, sufferers and carers outline the problems they have encountered along the way and suggest methods they have found helpful in restoring a sense of harmony to a troubled home. The do's and don'ts they have compiled may be useful reference points in what, for many, will be uncharted terrain. These particular carers and sufferers – all pioneers in their own ways – have the advantage of familiarity with a landscape they have spent many years mapping out. They now offer you the benefit of their experiences.

'Isolation is one of the hardest things to deal with,' says David Juggins whose wife, Sue, has suffered intermittently from depression for several years. 'When Sue was at her worst she lacked all motivation. She couldn't even bring herself to make a cup of tea. She was like a zombie, rocking from side to side. She wouldn't speak. She wouldn't use the telephone (which is her lifeline), she didn't want visitors and she didn't want to go out. It was all very worrying because at the back of your mind you have this fear that she'll commit suicide or something. I took time off work to look after her, but, even when I was at home, I had no idea what she might do.'

Communication under such circumstances is extremely difficult. After a tiring day at work, and an equally tiring time looking after Sue, David often wanted someone to talk to. But there was no one. Sue could not be blamed for being uncommunicative. That much he knew – 'that's what depression does to you, after all' – but this knowledge did little to help his isolation.

'Carers, especially men, have no one to confide in,' he says. 'If they go down to the pub the lads will say, "Oh, don't worry, she'll pull herself out of it", which is absolutely no help at all. Or they'll say, "Have another drink, it'll be OK".'

In other words no one is really listening to the carer's appeal for understanding. Listening takes some effort. It does not come naturally and, even for those who naturally feel the inclination to help, a very special kind of listening is needed if it is going to bear fruit. David is inclined to conclude gloomily that, 'unless you've experienced depression you've no idea what to expect at all. You don't know how to cope and you don't know how to help others cope, either.'

Carol understands the reaction completely. But she sees it from the other side. At the age of 40 she underwent a kind of breakdown for which she was treated with medication. The depression she experienced had very negative effects on her home life and on her husband whom she knows to be loving and supportive. 'I just felt myself withdrawing from life,' she says. 'I would wake up wondering what point there was in going on. I used to say to my husband, "I'm not the Carol you married". I knew I was driving him away from me and there was nothing I could do about it. I used to look at the helplessness in his eyes.'

The sheer bafflement of constantly looking after someone

who *looks* perfectly normal and able to look after him or herself is taxing enough. The mental and physical fatigue it causes is cumulative. 'Your whole life revolves around going to work in the morning,' says David, 'getting your job done as quickly as possible, then coming home and caring. And, while a lot of men are good at going out, earning the money and coming back, most of them are not prepared or able to look after the house as well.'

In this respect David and Sue are fortunate. David had been a bachelor all his life before he met Sue, then in her mid-forties and starting out again after a painful mid-life divorce. He had been used to shopping, cleaning, and cooking – things that most men, for one reason or another, often manage to keep at arm's length – and so was well placed to keep the home running smoothly.

Not all men are in his position. 'Other carers,' he says, 'may have problems. If the wife has looked after the running of the home and the husband has gone out to work expecting to come home and see his tea on the table, then you have a potential problem. The husband isn't equipped to do that sort of thing and, all of a sudden, without any preparation or training, he has to assume the role that the wife has been performing.'

He will have to look after any children, cooking for them, getting them ready for school. He will have to clean the house, balance the books – all chores difficult and demanding at the best of times but doubly so when there is no one there to share them with. And, of course, he has his wife to care for.

Different pressures build up in homes where the husband is depressed, but the pressures are just as hard to take. If he is the main breadwinner there will be the inescapable worries over money. Knowing in advance that 'this thing had better stop soon or we're not going to manage the mortgage repayments' is the worst possible way of inducing the sense of calm and patient compassion which is necessary for full health. The husband, moreover, may well feel guilty for his condition, even ashamed of it. He may reason that he is inadequate, feckless or irrespons-ible. Or simply that he has let the family down and everybody would be better off without him.

The fact is that, in a world where we all rely on each other to get by, *no one* is better off without anyone else.

Amid such understandable uncertainties and anxieties, how-ever, it is not surprising, as David Juggins puts it, that 'no matter what you do you don't feel appreciated'. What can happen next is that the closer a person is to another (whether to a partner, a child or a parent) the more that person feels rejected.

If people are not prepared for such reactions, which in the circumstances are quite natural, then they are likely to blame themselves all the more and, in a general mess of powerlessness, incomprehension, irritation and genuine affection, believe (quite mistakenly) that no solutions are possible. This is one of the worst conclusions to draw because negative thoughts are precisely what are NOT needed at moments like these.

But negative thoughts are quite natural, too. As Elisabeth Salisbury of The Samaritans puts it: 'There are so many things tied up in supporting a depressed person who is close to you. One of the things you're looking at is the death of your own hopes, and the limiting of your own horizons. What we can do as Samaritans is to reassure a sufferer that things will get better over time. Reassuring carers, who are desperate for the family member to get out of the depression, is damn difficult.'

But it is not impossible. The first step may lie in preparing carers for the unexpected problems they are likely to face. In practice, the 'limiting of horizons', for example, may mean being unable to plan family holidays – either because the sufferer is in no mood to concentrate on planning ahead when dealing with the present is painful enough, or because an expensive spring break in the Lake District may be a costly mistake if it coincides with a depressive mood.

'It would be impossible for us to get out the brochures,' says David Juggins, 'if Sue were in one of her depressions. You just have to accept restricted expectations. And this applies to social events, too. It's pointless trying to plan a Friday evening out when you can't be sure what mood a sufferer is going to be in.'

Very often this will mean that a carer will have to rearrange (or curtail) his or her own social life to fit in with a partner. And this can cause stress. But stress of that type is, to some degree, predictable. What many carers, by contrast, are not prepared for is the disruption that occurs when a sufferer is getting better. This is not a time when things automatically get back to normal and carers need to be warned.

One man, for instance, had compensated for his wife's inability to take part in their old social life by developing a new one. He had joined a local railway society and enjoyed the company of others as they talked about, restored and drove locomotives. Once his wife was out of her depression he found himself having to give up something in which he was now taking a lot of pleasure. Not surprisingly such demands put a great deal of strain on a marriage and, in some cases, can test a relationship to the limit.

Another man, similarly caring for a depressed partner, found himself having to take on the unfamiliar role of managing the family budget on reduced means. With considerable effort he was able to hit on a scheme which kept the family finances afloat in a choppy economic climate. When his wife got better he thought the financial situation would improve. In fact, it did the reverse. Returning to her old self with a renewed vigour for life she decided she needed new clothes, a change of scenery, new wallpaper in the living room, all the things, in other words, that she had been missing out on before. To no one's surprise the carefully controlled budget went askew and, although her husband was delighted to see her well again, he found his pleasure slightly dampened by the temporary downturn in the family finances.

David Juggins has seen all the permutations of upset that both the illness and the recovery can inflict. 'You wear yourself out caring,' he says with no trace of bitterness or ill feeling, 'and all the time your body's crying out for a rest. When the sufferer begins to get better you think, "thank goodness for that, now I'll get the rest I need". But it doesn't happen like that because when their mood improves they want to do all those things that they haven't been doing for months. So they're saying let's go for a day out here or the theatre there and all you can say is, "Hang on a minute; all I feel like doing is staying at home and pottering around. I'm washed out".'

It is precisely because carers can encounter such unpredictable situations that David Juggins helps to run a support group for them. 'We can share our experiences,' he says, 'and pool our knowledge. The doctors can tell us that the medication will take care of the depression. But they won't tell us how to take care of the home while our husbands and wives are swallowing the tablets.'

The group looks at the big problems and the small – on the basis that even small problems have to be confronted. Let his own experience speak for itself – highlighting, as it does, the countless minor adjustments a carer may have to make. What follows is one of those everyday problems many men (lacking a Grade A in domestic science) will be powerless to tackle.

Sue, his wife, was morose and off her food. Any other depressed person would probably be displaying similar symptoms. What should David, the concerned carer, do? He decided to prepare food that he had *specially chosen;* to serve up dishes that were *temptingly presented* – which was all very well for a man who knew, in the first place, how to cook a stew, prepare a salad, or poach an egg. For others (men, it has to be said) who lack even the basic skills of cookery such refinements are out of the question. What a support group can do, short of organising Cordon Bleu classes, is prepare the carer in advance for such demands and suggest, if it's possible, that he (just possibly she) get in a few tasty treats. This may seem like basic information but David knows that it can prove to be very useful in fostering the general sense of well-being that is so important to recovery.

Talking about the problem is not the only function the support group provides. It offers a network of helpers who can be called on to step in during a crisis. 'Carers need a break,' says David. 'In my case I would ask someone to come round to the house every Thursday evening while I went out to play badminton. I could thrash that shuttlecock around the court to my heart's content knowing that Sue was being looked after. And carers need to be able to have some time to themselves just to get their minds off things.'

This was the ploy Judy Lanham would use when looking after Paul at his worst. 'I have to confess that I frequently lost patience,' she says honestly of what was an intensely difficult period both for her and for her ten- and 12-year-old daughters. 'The girls were at school so they were out of it for most of the time but when they were at home they suffered from the tension in the household. We used to try to get out on Saturdays without Paul so that we could relax. That was the thing. In the house we could never relax. He was unpredictable. I suppose in a way I was never really aware of his pain in those days. I was too busy trying to keep life for everybody else on something like a normal footing. It didn't make me depressed. It made me angry. I suppose part of the problem was that my parents died over this period and Paul's behaviour was not at all helpful. I did however have some very supportive friends.'

Paul recognises the disruption his moods were causing the family but it is only with distance between him and the experience that he can now see it for what it was. 'I bitterly resented Judy taking the girls off at the time,' he remembers, 'but this was the only thing they could do. Carers need to develop a sense of self-preservation in order to keep going. The pressures on them are indescribable and people need to be told.'

'Perhaps the worst thing is that there can be a tendency for patients to pass their anger on to the carer. They want to offload their pain on to someone else. I was aware of inflicting unreasonable demands on the family. But there was nothing I could do about it at the time. Nothing. And there was no help we could get from either set of parents. None of them could handle it. My mother had had depression before and found it difficult to cope with; whereas, in my father's case, mental illness simply didn't fit in with his way of thinking.'

Joanna, who at 25 has come through the experience all the stronger for it, does not hide the pain Paul's condition dealt on the household. There was embarrassment at having a father who was different from all the rest; there was the hurt at seeing their parents shouting at each other when the pressure became too much to bear; and there was the sheer anguish of seeing their father, whom they loved and longed to be close to, behaving in a way which effectively distanced them from him. But she can also remember a significant turning point: 'Once we knew he was suffering from an illness we were able to accept it. And by just accepting it as a disorder like anything else we were able to learn to live with it.'

Acceptance and patience are not easily acquired but, in the care of depression, they are worth striving for. Together they give the carer two of the most powerful tools with which to construct the coping mechanisms necessary for long-term survival.

'One of our slogans in the group,' says David, 'is that there is light at the end of the tunnel. We can't promise you how long that tunnel is going to be but we can say you will come out of it.' They have seen enough people emerge into the daylight to be convinced of that. And David himself knows how dark that tunnel can sometimes be. He only has to look back at his wife's experience.

In many ways Sue's first depression had been predictable and had occurred at a point in life when all the danger signs were metaphorically flashing. She was a teacher in her mid-forties, in charge of a large nursery department in a busy and successful school. During the day she was under pressure at work and during the evening she returned to a marriage on the brink of collapse (not her subsequent marriage to David). She had teenaged children to look after and was feeling besieged on all sides.

'I used to push myself to the limits,' she recalls now, much chastened for the experience. 'I thought I was Superwoman. I had a big house with a big garden and a husband who was jetting abroad all the time.' Although she knew the marriage was in difficulties, neither partner had discussed it openly. So when her husband, who had been secretly buying his own house elsewhere and removing some of the contents of the family home to his new residence, told her that he was leaving, she was devastated.

She became acutely depressed and suffered three major bouts of depression before her marriage of 22 years finally ended in divorce. 'I was suicidal,' she remembers. 'I had no interest in dressing properly. I wouldn't wash. I lost all confidence. I took an overdose. The whole thing had a disastrous effect on the children but there was no way I could control it. I simply crumpled. I could not cope and, although my husband arranged for people to come round and look after me, neither could he. His reaction was to go away, to go abroad. My black mood lasted from the moment I got up until the moment I went to bed. I couldn't stop crying and it was more than I could do to make a cup of coffee.'

In time, the depression eased enough for life to resume. Life was not to return to as before – the divorce had seen to that – but it was to carry on as Sue bought herself a smaller house and began again.

During this gradual period of adjustment she met David. They married but within three weeks of the marriage Sue had relapsed and had to be admitted into hospital. Like any concerned partner David was immediately supportive. But, as time wore on, he realised that he was unprepared for the specific demands of this particular illness. Heart trouble, an ulcer, varicose veins he could have understood. But depression, well, that was a new one on him.

Little did he realise that he was about to start learning very fast. 'I didn't really know what was happening,' he says. 'There was no one to advise me. The doctors just said she would keep taking the tablets until she got better. And as for when she would get better . . . well, we'd just have to trust to luck.'

Fortunately David, who describes himself as a 'fairly placid sort of bloke', proved also to be a patient and reassuring sort of husband – qualities which complemented the domestic skills he had honed down as a bachelor. Although he would probably be the first to admit that he made mistakes along the way, he was careful **to back up any verbal reassurance with a practical gesture**. So he would arrange, for example, to telephone from work at fixed hours during the day. 'This was very important,' he says now, 'because if I had arranged to phone at 12 o'clock and I phoned at 5 to or 5 past, Sue wouldn't pick up the phone.' Things had to be regular, ordered and reliable.

When Sue was in the worst of the depression, holding on to the light-at-the-end-of-the-tunnel principle was not easy. In fact, at first, doing so was more an act of faith. As he became more familiar with the pattern of the attacks he was able to hold on to it with more and more conviction. One thing that David noticed was the fact that the depressive bouts always came to an end after three months or so. He had no reason to suppose, therefore, that they would continue beyond that time. And they didn't. That knowledge, confirmed by many of the other depressed people he has worked with, was a lifeline.

That there *was* light at the end of the tunnel was an inescapable fact. Sure, the phrase may have suffered a little from overuse but the cliché *was true*. It was an immense relief. Armed with this piece of reassurance, he saw that his patience was being rewarded. And as he took an active interest in the pattern of Sue's depression he was able, from a perspective of knowledge, to reassure her all the more and to help her to deal with things.

For instance, he noticed that the recovery period (towards the end of the customary three months) began with the same distinct signs with which the depression had begun. But, whereas the depression signalled itself with negative signs – disrupted sleep, increasing fatigue and lethargy – the recovery was marked by positive improvements which all but the most vigilant would have missed.

David was able to build on these improvements and to encourage Sue to make more. For her part, thinking herself still in the grip of depression, she might dismiss the encouragement and say something like, 'I'm not getting any better. This is hopeless.' He, however, could say, 'Look, today you made two cups of coffee whereas yesterday you only made one. You're doing fine.' She might not *feel* convinced but she could not argue with the facts. And, little by little, the facts would accumulate to make a cognitive case for improvement which she would be in a position to accept when the depression lifted.

Such reinforcement is important to people in depression. When they are down they will ignore all their good qualities and see only the worst aspects of their personality. If a relative or friend can focus attention on positive aspects of the sufferer's achievements then that sufferer, even if only subconsciously, will begin to think that he or she is not such a hopeless case after all.

It is a good idea to write down some of the day's achievements on a piece of paper – dated and timed to give the facts the force of objective evidence – and to confront a sufferer with the findings.

'No, you did get up early. Early for you that is. Yesterday you got up at 11am. Today . . .'

'You ARE good with the kids. Sarah was telling me the other day . . .'

'Look, everybody says you are a caring person. What about the time . . .'

'You can cook. Peter said that the last time he came here he'd never tasted better . . .'

'But you can play the piano. Not everybody can. And Sarah said she wished SHE . . .'

'Have you seen the state of Alan's garden? And that's when he's well. If you were . . .'

David and Sue's group exists to stress the positive. There have been success stories by the score. A person descended into the pit, a partner shared partially in the gloom, but together they were able to emerge into the light.

David remembers one particular case where the wife had suffered recurrent depression for years. The husband had stood by, helping where he could, until a crisis in the family turned the tables. He had a mental breakdown and was himself plunged into despondency. She was now forced into the carer's role. 'The people in the group were able to support her through what was a pretty harrowing time,' he recalls. 'She would say things like, "He's not the husband I married. We may as well split up." The physical side of things had gone and she felt isolated and unable to cope.' What members of the group could do was to remind her what she had gone through and to compare his experience with hers. Just as her depression had lifted so, too, they said to her repeatedly, would his depression go. And it did. With the result that they are stronger as a couple now than they were before.

Carol, too, has oscillated between extremes of emotion but has reached a workable compromise. She loves her husband (her second) and reckons that without him she would not be able to cope. He is a kind and loving man who persuades her that life is worth living but, at her worst, she has gone to her doctor and said, 'If you were a vet I'd ask you to put me down. This depression is worse than any physical illness and I can't see an end in sight when I'm down in this pit.'

Carol attends David and Sue's support group so, clearly, despite what she feels in her darkest moments, she has had the courage to take a leap of faith and to say, 'Though I cannot yet see the sun, I know that it will rise.'

'Patience,' says David, 'is essential. And you also have to listen to what people are saying.' There are, however, ways and ways of listening.

All too often, listening means simply 'hearing' what's been said and responding with anything from a grunt to a yawn. Listening, *really* listening, implies taking an active interest, wanting to know that little bit more about the experiences and the feelings of the person who is doing the talking. It is called empathy, 'fellow feeling' for short, the ability to identify oneself mentally and emotionally with the person who is talking to you. It is a means of understanding (or trying to, at least) what people are really going through.

The story Carol tells illustrates how NOT to do it:

❛Through therapy I've learnt to understand how I've been brought up. My dad, for example, was always an anxious person. If anything went wrong, my reactions were to panic, cry, or run away. I never felt good enough. One day I'd be fine, the next I'd be terrible. In fact, it changed from hour to hour. From minute to minute. One minute I'm up, the next I'm down. I got up this morning and I could have cried. I don't know why. I'm the kind of person who invites someone round for dinner on Friday and gets so wound up by Wednesday that I have to cancel it all. So I start to talk to people about this and my dad says, "Never mind". Now, that really works me up. Because I DO mind. ❜

The first mistake Carol's father made in this particular encounter was basic. A carer must realise that a depressed person is in pain. The depression hurts just as much as a toothache hurts. To say 'don't worry' or 'never mind' about a toothache is absurd. When you have toothache you DO mind. Just as Carol minded.

What her father (or anybody else) should have done was to accept the pain Carol felt. From there he should have tried to understand how she felt. And how better to begin the process of understanding than to ask. Merely asking is enough to show the barest minimum of care. So the above conversation could have been acted out quite differently.

> *Carol:* 'I'm going to have to cancel Friday night.'
> *Carer:* 'Why's that?'
> *Carol:* 'Oh, I just don't feel I can face it.'
> *Carer:* 'Why not, do you think?'
> *Carol:* 'I can't face talking to anybody.'
> *Carer:* 'Are you up to cooking?'
> *Carol:* 'Yes, I could probably manage that. But making conversation's just too much hard work right now.'
> *Carer:* 'Well, get Bill to do the entertaining. You can keep your head down in the kitchen. He can explain you're not up to it.'
> *Carol:* 'But I just feel so miserable.'
> *Carer:* 'It's getting you down, isn't it?'
> *Carol:* 'Yes.'
> *Carer:* 'Does anything take your mind off it?'
> *Carol:* 'Well, not really but . . .'

The imaginary dialogue ends on a hopeful note as Carol begins to come out of her shell and, **encouraged and supported**, she starts to explore her own pain with a concerned friend. Real life is not always like that, of course, and getting through to a depressed person is often a long haul with few apparent signs that progress is being made.

But the principle of 'concerned listening' stays good. Preaching a sermon to someone or delivering a stirring speech about how bright the future will be are of no practical use to a person in depression. Indeed, the tactics may be counterproductive and serve only to deepen the isolation.

Depression is a kind of journey through a dark wood. It is bleak, hard, and lonely – with the possibility of taking turnings that lead further into the undergrowth. It is a journey that a person giving the stirring sermon or the cheery advice is effectively refusing to make with the sufferer. Sure, that person has a map and all the directions to hand and is only too willing to pass the information on. But however much information or guidance he imparts, he makes it clear, from his attitude, that he is planning to stay put while the sufferer presses on.

The compassionate listener says something rather different. He or she says, 'Look, we have no maps. There are no guide books to help us. But why don't we set off together and see if we can get through? We may take a couple of wrong turnings along the way but, if we do, we'll take them together and, who knows, we may find ourselves on a pathway out of here sooner than we thought.'

This is a lengthy commitment for a carer. For a spouse, it may be a lifetime's work. Then again, it may last only a few weeks or months as the sufferer enters a periodic bout of depression. What carers can often do best during these times is simply to be present until the worst passes. The husband can reassure his depressed wife that she is making progress; the wife can suggest to her depressed husband that they *both* follow the doctor's orders and take some exercise together; and family and friends can send cards and letters to a sufferer, constantly reassuring (in person, in print, or on the telephone) that their thoughts are never far away.

The results of this kind of care are not always visible but they are cumulative. At times a sufferer will appear to fly off the handle with a carer or to take out the depression or frustration on the very person who is trying to help. This can be particularly hard. Under such circumstances carers should be encouraged to persevere and not to feel that outbursts of temper or irritation are personally meant. With a little insight and a lot of patience they can eventually learn to deflect the anger and to respond with kindness and calm.

If the presence of a supportive partner is invaluable during the dark times it is an occasion of joy and celebration when the happiness returns. One sufferer recalls how he felt when he was restored to health:

❛ I remember standing at a bus stop one morning and thinking how all the darkness and the greyness had lifted. It was as if I'd been looking at the world through a sooty window for all those months. Now somebody had come along and wiped the window clean and the light just streamed in. I'll never forget it. **'**

To have another person sharing in that pleasure is guaranteed to strengthen any relationship. And in many cases it will have a wonderfully restorative effect, cancelling out past pain at a stroke and bringing two (or more) people into a real sense of communion. Paul and Judy, and daughters Joanne and Elizabeth, for example made it through:

Joanne: We paid a price for Dad's depression. We were weekly boarders and coming home wasn't nice at weekends. The atmosphere was tense and fraught.

Judy: Paul and I sometimes had arguments. Fights, really. Throwing bottles, that sort of thing.

Joanne: Slamming doors.

Paul: On the other hand I remember you storming out one night in winter in your nightdress.

Judy: They were tense times and one draws a veil over them. But we've come through it all more or less intact. And I think that, although we put up with a lot, it wasn't as much as Paul was having to go through.

Paul: I like being told that but I don't believe it. I think we're closer now than we've ever been.

This is *one* success story. But there are many more. David Juggins, who works with carers, has heard such stories and seen for himself that depression need not stretch a family to breaking point. What he and those in his group do is to encourage patience and acceptance. There will be times when a carer needs to be actively reassuring and positively encouraging; equally there will be times when he or she will have to stand back, to allow sufferers to be solitary and silent for a while.

During these periods a husband or a wife will need the patience to withdraw – perhaps for an hour, perhaps for an evening, or for a few days – and, in that time, to feel neither rejected nor ignored. Obviously if there is any indication of impending self-harm or of suicide then a carer will have to seek professional help and may have to ask others to intervene. Otherwise, all that may be necessary is to keep an eye on things from a discreet distance until the sufferer feels ready to make contact again.

Those engaged in that difficult, selfless, baffling, frustrating, infuriating but ultimately loving task of caring for another human being might fruitfully learn something from the combined experiences of the Depression Alliance which has compiled a rough and ready guide for carers.

Things carers should avoid

- Don't try to jolly sufferers along. Telling them to pull themselves together is pointless. They neither choose to be nor wish to remain in the depressed state. So they would pull themselves together if they could. But they can't.
- Don't tell them they are imagining it all. The experience is real for them and the pain is often acute. Like any illness it has to run its course. But like any other illness many of its symptoms can be alleviated.
- Don't be critical. Depressed people are sensitive and easily upset. Even slight criticism can plunge them into the depths of despair.
- Don't suggest that they themselves are to blame for their state of mind. They may well be feeling guilty in any case and also painfully aware of the demands they are making on those around them.
- Don't try to force them into action. Offer gentle, persistent encouragement and stimulation.
- Don't interfere with treatment that a sufferer finds helpful. Negative remarks like, 'Don't take those pills, they won't do you any good', or 'What do you want to go and see a shrink for?' will further undermine confidence and deepen confusion.
- Don't ever give up. There *is* light at the end of the tunnel.

Positive action carers should take

- Encourage a person to talk to a doctor if the condition persists.

- Try to show that you want to help and understand.
- Remind sufferers every day that depression is a temporary state and that the vast majority of people will get better in time.
- Encourage them to take some form of exercise. Walking and swimming are generally accessible to most people – whatever their age and physical condition.
- Continue to remind yourself that you are not wasting your time and effort.
- Remember to look after yourself. Continue to keep channels of communication open with fellow carers. You need reassurance, too!

With experience, carers will learn to play a situation by ear – judging when it is advisable to get involved and when it is better to pull back. In all this, however, it is worth reminding oneself that the best kind of help is that which enables sufferers to help themselves. Any decisions they make *for* themselves and any answers they find *by* themselves are more likely to be effective in the long term than any solutions proposed by someone else – however well meaning that someone else is.

And bear in mind that there is life beyond depression. Moods will lift just as the sky will clear. In the depth of her own despair Sue Juggins would never have believed it. But, now restored to health, she is forced to accept that it is indeed true. And anyone in temporary despair might just take heart from what she (who has been there herself) has to say: 'I want to live life to the full. And those people I know who have had depression feel the same. They don't want to miss a moment.'

7

Finding the Strength for Recovery

Throughout this book depression has been consistently compared and contrasted with physical illness. True, the average person with no experience of the condition is likely not to see the comparison, and to dismiss it with a remark such as, 'Oh, it's all in the mind' – as if the mind were somehow immune from pain. But the sufferer knows otherwise.

To stay with that comparison, there is a phrase often used during convalescence from everyday sickness: 'When you get your strength back,' a carer will frequently say, 'we'll go on a shopping expedition, or we'll go off for the weekend, or we'll redecorate the house or whatever . . .' It's always 'when you've got your strength back'. The same holds true for many types of depression. In these cases the strength that needs to be recovered is of a different kind but it is just as important in the journey back to health.

'One theory of depression expounded a few years ago,' says consultant psychiatrist, Sally Pidd, 'involved so-called "learned helplessness". If you were in a situation in which you felt there was nothing you could do to help yourself, so the theory went, then you might have a tendency to become depressed. So what people treating the condition had to do was to work out ways of increasing the patient's sense of power, their sense of some sort of mastery over even quite simple things.'

It is possible for the patient to help in the process, too. This is what David found in his own case. David was in his early 40s and living alone following a traumatic divorce. Although, by day, he was holding down a responsible job in the City, by night he found himself feeling increasingly isolated in his flat. In the course of two years' psychotherapy with an understanding counsellor he was able to get at what he thought was the root of his depression and anxiety.

All his life he had felt alone. Although his parents had given him every material advantage, sacrificing much to send him first to a private school and then to university where he excelled, they had neglected him emotionally. His father, a policeman, had worked long and irregular hours and had rarely played with him as a child. His mother, too, went out to work and was never at home when David returned from school.

In time, although David felt miserable coming back to a cold house and preparing a solitary tea for himself in front of the TV, he adjusted to the constant state of loneliness. He had friends, was popular at school, and seemed outwardly confident. Inside, however, the sense of isolation was slowly working its corrosive effect. Despite the bold exterior he was desperately insecure and, after a series of unsatisfactory relationships at university, he married the first woman who seemed to promise him unconditional affection and security.

The marriage did not last and when he found himself suddenly divorced in mid life he felt the old familiar sense of loneliness returning. Going back to an empty flat brought back all the old images and sensations of the past – the solitary tea, the chilly house, and the vague feeling of abandonment. Accordingly, he stayed out in the evenings more and more, spending far more than was wise on drinks, meals out, and all the other entertainments that would keep the dreaded moment of return at bay. Eventually, through therapy, he was able to examine not only the root of his loneliness but the nature of it as well. And he discovered that a large component was fear, fear of not being able to cope by himself, fear of his own powerlessness in a basically unfriendly world.

By talking through his childhood experiences he found that the lack of a strong paternal influence on his life had propelled him increasingly to his mother who doted on him and did everything for him. The apple of his mother's eye, he managed to get his own way in life merely by asking for all his needs to be met. And since he worked hard at school, avoided trouble, kept any adolescent trauma to himself and was such a credit to the family, his mother duly obliged. But in meeting all his needs she allowed him to 'learn powerlessness'.

The results were damaging – though she herself had no intention of causing any damage and would have been horrified to discover that she had. When he looked at himself now as a man he saw an essentially frightened and lonely child and this, he concluded had been at the root of what he called 'a chronic low-level depression which seems to have been with me for as long as I can remember'.

What he needed to learn was that he could exercise some control over his life again. It was not an easy process but his therapist suggested he might start with the flat. If it seemed cheerless to him, why shouldn't he try to brighten it up a bit? What about a few pictures on the wall? Why not try making the place comfortable and staying in two or three nights a week to read or to listen to some music? By encouraging him to go into the difficult experience and to master it (as opposed to walking away from the experience and being under its control) his therapist was teaching him an invaluable (though initially painful) lesson. Like the damsel 'in distress' in Uccello's painting of St George and the Dragon, David was able to face his own demons and, if not to slay them, at least to tame them and to live at peace with them. He, like the serene and apparently fragile woman in the painting, was in control and he, like her, held the lead connected to the collar of the dragon which now dutifully did as it was commanded.

David painted the flat, mastered the arts of washing up and hoovering, and started to find that he was building a secure base from which to start his life again. This time, however, it was to be a life over which he, to his great psychological relief, had some sort of mastery. 'It's not easy,' he says, 'but at least I've learnt the technique now. I still get depressed at times but I've learnt to spot when I'm heading for a low and sort of keep my head down until it passes. Then the first thing I do is go for a run or read a book or invite someone round to the flat for a meal. Anything so long as I'm actually DOING something rather than giving in to the old feelings of helplessness. All my life I've behaved as a boy really. I suppose I'm just beginning to grow up. And although things get a bit hard at times I feel I'm getting stronger and stronger. That constant background feeling of gnawing, aching depression has vanished. Sure, I get low now and then but I feel I have the strength to see things through and life is getting a lot better for it.'

Nick, the writer, is learning to take the same evasive action himself:

> ❛ I have to try to keep myself occupied. It's hard to do – and that's when I lie in bed all the time. But I know that's when I'm at my worst. In bed I'm doing nothing, just stewing in it but if I can push myself into doing something then I find it's OK. Anything that keeps me occupied, going for a run, tidying the flat, makes me feel better. ❜

Dr Pidd has noticed that persuading patients that they can do things for themselves has a therapeutic effect. The degree to which she and others can be successful varies enormously but the principle remains the same. 'Some people will maintain that nothing ever goes right for them,' she says, 'and so they've stopped trying to do things. If you can suggest that they actually take some constructive steps to do something – even though they may feel they are being rebuffed – then that can be of benefit. We actually run assertiveness classes for people and quite a few of our patients who are depressed benefit from them. That's because part of their depressed state is their lack of power.'

The Depression Alliance newsletter retells the story of an American journalist accompanying his friend to the newsstand one day. There his friend asks courteously for a paper, politely hands over the money and receives a gruff response in return as the vendor slams the paper down in front of him.

'Is he always as rude as that?' asks the journalist.

'Yes. Every day.'

'Why are you so polite then?'

'Because I don't want him deciding how I'm going to behave.'

Very often such self-assertiveness is a feature of a strong sense of self-esteem which, in turn, has been fostered by careful, attentive parents during childhood. Equally often, depression is a feature of lack of self-worth and the corresponding sense of powerlessness that attends it.

It would, of course, be wonderful if the phenomenon of depression could be reduced to a single satisfactory equation. 'Powerlessness plus lack of self-worth equal depression' would then have the same revelatory force as, say, Einstein's $E = mc^2$. But things are not as simple as that and extracting a consistent quantum theory of depression from an infinite series of variables is the subject of a lifetime's (probably fruitless) research.

As Dr Pidd puts it: 'A lot of depressed mood is to do with poor self-esteem but it's difficult to know whether people have a poor view of themselves and so are depressed, or whether they first get depressed – which in turn distorts their view of themselves. 'I suppose if you grow up in a situation where you're affirmed and people tell you that you're worth while, you stand a much better chance of having positive self-worth than if you're always being ignored. I think parental figures are the key ones.'

Nuala, who is 37 and who has worked intermittently in the music business, reckons that this was the root of her depression:

❝ Most of the family did well academically and I didn't seem to prove myself. My grandparents were schoolteachers and there's a long history of Degrees and God knows what in the family. Everything was geared towards academic success and somehow I didn't fit. It wasn't so much that I was incapable, it was just that I had decided I was. When I was 13 I was sent to a different secondary school than the one my brothers and sisters were sent to and I developed quite a serious inferiority complex. It's only since I've been away from the family that I've discovered that I can do things and that I'm not such a pea-brain after all. ❞

But such an experience, though common in itself, is not sufficient to explain depression completely and Sally Pidd is wary of concluding (from this or any other experience) that any quantum theory is at hand. 'Some people have lousy parents who do nothing to build up their self-esteem and yet they get by. They can come across a teacher at school, maybe, or someone who injects a positive sense of self-worth in them and they are really turned round.'

To say, then, that parental encouragement is vital to mental health and that the lack of such encouragement provokes depression is only part of the picture – an important part, maybe, but only one part of a picture that is very large indeed.

Research carried out by Professor George Brown and his colleagues at the Department of Social Policy and Social Science at Royal Holloway College in London suggests that other key features in the onset of depression are loss, humiliation and entrapment. The loss may, of course, be through bereavement. But it may be something as abstract as the loss of a cherished belief – a religious faith or political ideology, for example, or a belief in fidelity, rudely shattered when a partner has an affair.

In the research, 'humiliation' was used to describe the effects of an event which has somehow devalued a person – either in relation to others or to self. This might occur in the case of a divorced mother being told by her 14-year-old daughter that she wants to live with her father; a girl being told by her boyfriend that he does not want to have an exclusive sexual relationship; most cases of admitted infidelity; a single mother being criticised by a magistrate for failing to pay a fine incurred by a teenaged son.

'Entrapment' involved the perception by people in difficult circumstances that their ways of escape were blocked. One example quoted was that of someone being told that the condition of a paralysed and bedridden husband would not improve. All these cases of loss, of humiliation, and of entrapment (conditions which will often overlap) may be accompanied by varying degrees of helplessness, powerlessness and defeat.

Now, while it is by no means assured that regaining strength and control will automatically banish depression for good, rediscovering a sense of mastery over potentially depressing events will almost certainly have a beneficial effect. The fact is that being a victim is extremely debilitating. One is, by definition, on the receiving end of things. And it is very tiring constantly to have to deal with whatever life seems to be dishing out at the time. It is far better to be able to filter out some of its more damaging side-effects at source. Having some sort of control over life's events regulates the cumulative stress they can generate.

What is more, events over which one may seem to have very little control can, if viewed in a positive frame of mind, be mastered in the end. A typical and nowadays very common example is unemployment which will often remove the sense of purpose from a person's life and lower his or her spirits. Loss of status, loss of direction, loss of promise, and loss of income can all trigger bouts of depression and, as a growing number of people know to their cost, frequently do.

In Dr Pidd's experience women fare much better than men in this category of life event. 'In my experience of working in an area of high unemployment,' she says, 'women can often find another role in life – frequently to do with the children. Unemployment for them isn't the be-all and end-all of things. Whereas men who are made redundant often lose the only thing that gives them a sense of value and purpose.'

Expectations of high achievement also mean that men are reluctant to take what they consider demeaning or unsuitable jobs. Women, on the other hand, seem likely to be more flexible in their approach to work on offer and may, in recessionary times, be paradoxically better placed to act as breadwinners – if their husbands or partners do not find the prospect too threatening.

Jonathan, for example, who attends a self-help group for depressed people in London is in his late 30s and has a job as a local government administrator. He says insecurity is one of the contributory factors to his depression and, asked what might go some way to lifting his mood, replies unequivocally:

❛ Having a secure future financially. Having a job for life and a feeling that I'm going somewhere. I don't want a lot of money. I would just like to think that in ten or twenty years I'd still be working; that I could be in a job, do well at it, and know that I'd be in it until retirement. But there isn't that kind of security any more. That stability has gone and so has a meaning to life. ❜

What is necessary in these circumstances is to develop a meaningful life independent of paid employment. It is, of course, far easier said than put into practice. And Dr Pidd is well aware of this. 'There are an awful lot of people in this recession who have lost their job,' she says, 'but not all of them become depressed.

So I suppose you can look at what made this person crash into depression and ask whether there are any factors in his life which are missing. Would it help, for example, to develop some meaningful hobbies or deploy the skills he already has in voluntary work. This is all pie in the sky when you're depressed because you just don't feel like doing those things. But if the reality is that people are not going to get a job then it's best to draw a line and say that life is not just about working. And here having a supportive partner or family to say, "It's no big deal. We'll survive" is enormously helpful.'

Simon Armson of The Samaritans knows from experience that unemployment puts enormous strains on people. He and his colleagues have often taken calls from those on the edge of despair because of it. He knows, too, that he cannot offer that distressed caller a job. But still he continues believing he can offer real comfort. How?

'One of the things that might help an unemployed man to feel better,' he says, 'is to allow him to be able to express how he feels about not having a job and have those feelings accepted. He may then go on to realise that not having a job in the way he had previously had a job is not the most important thing to him any more. Possibly a senior executive who's lost a job may have a very narrow view about what kind of future employment options are acceptable.

'Maybe, by talking through their feelings and by examining what it is that really matters to them, they can reposition their sights and aim for something they can achieve. The object of the process is to help people reach a conclusion for themselves. It may take a long time. It may mean going round in lots of circles and up lots of blind alleys but eventually the important thing will be for that person to say, "Well I suppose I just have to accept that that's the way it is." And for a lot of people that process of acceptance is a release in itself. They can then give themselves permission not to continue to strive for something which is inaccessible.'

The value of this approach is incalculable. For some, of course – those suffering from severe chemical or electrical imbalances of the brain, for whom medication is thought the only answer – such talk will be of limited use. But for those who have been incapacitated by feelings of powerlessness, the knowledge that they can have a stake in their own future can be immensely healing.

As Simon Armson puts it: 'Our philosophy is really based on the notion that people are in control of their own destiny. No one is going to take away their rights in that respect. Or, indeed, their responsibility. We are not there as the therapist or the doctor or anyone in a position of power. We are there as the enabler and the supporter. In that way the power remains with the individual and the power can be allowed to grow and to develop.'

An experience common to the majority of people with depression is the inability to see the future with any kind of conviction. They lack, in a word, hope. 'Part of the role of any professional or of any helping organisation,' says Sally Pidd, 'is, in some way, to instil hope. To convince people that there *is* a point in going on. When I am treating people I am basically optimistic that we will eventually work out a strategy or a treatment that will get people better. So part of my job is to instil the hope that although everything may look appallingly black now, at some time in the future a patient will not feel like this. And it often helps people to know that you have seen a lot of other people who have got better.'

Dr Pidd knows that such reassurance is of limited value in severe cases of depression. If people have a biological depression, she says, with deficiencies in the transmitter substances in the brain, then it is unlikely that talk or deep analysis will make much difference. As a psychiatrist, she would then consider medical intervention. 'However,' she says, 'there is a large group of people who don't have that sort of depression, whose depression, if they analyse it, is a lot to do with their upbringing, their early relationships, and their failed relationships. Therefore looking introspectively may actually be very beneficial for them.'

For many people, merely understanding how they have arrived at their depression is a useful means of transcending it. They now have a reason for feeling as they do and are thus in a position to address it. As they begin to come out of depression there are practical things they can do to consolidate the new-found strength that a proper sense of self-awareness may bestow.

According to Dr Pidd, it is useful to borrow from the

principles that Alcoholics Anonymous have established, chief among which, she says, is 'to take one day at a time. I talk to people about just surviving today. And that can give people a sense of achievement. It's a question of breaking things down into manageable chunks.'

Dr Pidd has the advantage of being able to take the longer view of a patient's depression, to be able to see that over a period of a month, say, there has been a definite improvement in the condition. The patient, by contrast, seeing little visible improvement from day to day, is too close to his or her depression to feel that there has been any progress.

She will ask a series of questions about apparently very simple things: 'How much of an effort was it to get up today?'; 'Did you get any real pleasure from anything this week?'; 'Have you been able to watch television?' and write down their responses. At a subsequent session she can ask similar questions and compare the relative answers. In this way she is in a position to confront patients with the evidence of their improvement. 'These may seem quite small things,' she says, 'but you keep on pressing people until you get quite a list of things that indicate real improvement. Then, of course, people will say, "But I don't feel like that every day." To which you can reply, "It doesn't matter. You've felt some of these things which you didn't feel before." '

Those coming out of depression might find similar exercises helpful:

- Keep a diary of improvements you have noticed in your condition. Write down all the achievements, however small, you think you have made. Make a note of things that have given you pleasure or made you smile. Note down sights or sounds or smells you have experienced.
- Make a list of things you want to have done by the end of the day and tick them off as you complete them.
- Try to take your thoughts off yourself and direct your efforts occasionally to other people and other things. Can you look after a friend's pet for a day? Are you able to make tea or a slice of toast for a friend or partner? Do you have a garden or a plant to tend? Can you throw out bread for the birds and watch them feeding?

- Take physical exercise, even if it involves nothing more than walking to the end of the garden and back. Try to get outdoors for at least a few minutes every day.
- Don't expect miracles. Be content with slow steady progress.
- Don't be downhearted if you fail to live up to your good intentions. Two or three things missed out from your list of daily achievements is not the end of the world. Press on regardless, noticing only what you HAVE done, not what you haven't.
- Make plans. For a real or imaginary holiday; for a celebration supper; for a day out. You may not actually go on the holiday or cook the supper but THINK about doing so.
- Think back to when you have been happy and say to yourself, 'I was happy then and I will be happy again. I was well then and some day – I can't be completely sure when – I will be well again.'

In all this the cardinal virtue is patience. 'People rarely get better in a straight line,' says Dr Pidd. 'Sometimes they do. If you give people a course of ECT when they're profoundly depressed and they respond to it, the response can be absolutely dramatic. You can have someone who was almost mute one week and who is eating and drinking the next, absolutely right as rain. But most people don't get better that quickly. In fact, in a way, the worse and more biological someone's depression is, the better the recovery. With a biological depression you've just got to reverse the process somehow and people get better, whereas if you've got something that's loaded with life events you've got more to overcome.'

What some of the practical exercises may help people to see is the general upward progress of their condition. There will almost certainly be ups and downs as a person comes out of a depressed mood but, by keeping some kind of written record, that person can be convinced that the underlying movement is upwards. Noting that the pattern or the quality of sleep has improved, noting that concentration has got better or that a person's appetite has picked up are all tangible reminders that recovery is under way.

8

Convalescence: 'Only Connect'

Depression at its most severe is a maximum security prison, and those people who are depressed are Category A prisoners with no licence to wander beyond the perimeter fence and no freedom of association within it. In this state of solitary confinement the condemned man or woman spends lonely nights and tormented days. Contact with the outside world is nil. Isolation is total. Depression does that.

The very worst cases will be referred to psychiatrists like Sally Pidd who calculates that most of those with sustained depression will not be back to full functioning in under six months. Even so, to her trained eye there will be signs that improvement is under way and these she can pass on to the patient. When people remark, with growing degrees of impatience and desperation, that their condition is not improving she can reassure them that, yes, objectively it is. 'And,' says Dr Pidd, 'when you can sense that people are on the way up it is helpful to be able to say, "Look, it's a slow process but you *are* getting better." '

When this happens the patient's 'incarceration', while not yet at an end, undergoes a crucial modification. The 'prisoner' is metaphorically moved to another wing of the jail and told that he or she is to be allowed visitors. And isolation, which is perhaps the defining feature of depression, gives way to a measure of contact with the outside world. As the condition of the patient slowly improves so, too, does the capacity to engage with others. And as the person feels able to rejoin the human race, so the condition improves. With that, the spiral of decline is reversed and begins to turn, at last, in a positive direction.

Sally Pidd has hopeful stories to tell. She once treated a young woman who was severely disturbed with a depressive psychosis. She heard voices which she believed were coming from the devil and became convinced that something evil was physically invading her body. At first Dr Pidd thought the condition might be part of a schizophrenic illness but eventually she concluded that it was an aspect of a severe depression.

Together they discussed (as one aspect of a vastly more complex treatment) the possibility of her attending a drama therapy group in an effort to build up her confidence with other people again. With some nervousness she went along but after two weeks was on the brink of giving up. On the third week, however, having persevered against the odds she was able to join in fully and made a positive contribution to the group.

From here a healthy upward spiral began. A measure of confidence gained, she then expressed to Dr Pidd the desire 'to do something ordinary but useful'. Between them they came up with the idea of doing a word processing course so that, when the young woman was well enough to resume her university course (which the illness had temporarily interrupted), she would have a definite skill to hand.

What complemented any other medical treatment was the positive contact the woman was having with everyday society. No longer was she completely a prisoner of her condition. From utter solitude in an isolated cell she was, as it were, able to transfer to an open prison. While her depressed mood prevented her, for the time being, from taking full satisfaction in the world around her she was being gradually prepared for re-entry into everyday life by her increasing (and increasingly useful) contact with it. The notion of usefulness is important.

Dr Pidd is well aware of the need to be practical and realistic in the choice of an activity that will help a patient rejoin the society of others. 'I know what we have available here in the hospital in terms of occupational therapy,' she says, 'so I often suggest they consider a pottery group or a lunch club (where patients prepare meals for themselves) – simply because that's what's on offer.' She knows the potential problem inherent in such suggestions. They are, quite simply, not always suitable. 'Often men have never done anything like pottery in their life.

And if they're not going to do it when they're well, they're
certainly not going to do it when they're ill.'

Similarly, of the well-intentioned lunch club she says, 'We
often try to encourage people to get back to doing things like
cooking because when people are depressed they don't
always eat properly. But if you have a male chauvinist type who
doesn't know how to open a tin, then it's not always a good idea
to choose the very moment he's coming out of a depression to
persuade him to try.'

Choosing a *suitable* activity is important. It needs to be one
which gives a sense of purpose and goes with the grain of the
person involved – not against natural inclinations and aptitudes.
Arranging flowers in the church will be suitable for some sufferers coming out of depression but it will be wholly unsuitable for
others. Helping to run a club or a voluntary society will be a
productive undertaking for some people whereas, for others,
merely being around to lend a hand is enough.

The satisfaction gained from working with others is extremely
important in the process of recovery from depression. It is not
simply a question of giving the sufferer 'something to do'. Its
importance goes much deeper than that and involves rebuilding
a person's sense of usefulness and of purpose in life.

> ❛People ask me how I got rid of depression and I say,
> "Simple". I became the Chairman of Depression Alliance.
> Some time ago when I first joined DA I was asked to chair a
> meeting. I said I couldn't possibly do it. I thought I just wasn't
> up to it. They persisted and I relented but I did a deal. I said I
> would chair things until the next AGM. I'm still doing it five
> years later! ❜
>
> *Paul Lanham*

Retired men who are depressed have a problem in that most
voluntary jobs seem designed for women but the problem need
not be insoluble. There are countless other examples of constructive work – not all of it obvious. Peter is in his early fifties and
was invalided out of a high-powered clerical job directly as a
result of his increasing depressions. Medication and hospitalisa-
tion were effective in dealing with the worst of his condition but,

once his moods had stabilised, he needed an activity which would prevent him slipping back into the gloom.

The choice he made is, at first sight, rather implausible. Walking into his house one is surprised to see stacks of telephone directories in one corner of the room and, in another, piles of leaflets advertising a local Tandoori restaurant. Strange, one thinks initially, that this former managerial supremo seems to have turned his home into a waste-paper collection depot. All is not, however, as it seems. Peter has a part-time job delivering the local freesheet (which includes the Tandoori ad) to houses in the local area. The regular contact that this allows him to make with other people is, he believes, vital in building up what self-esteem and self-worth he had lost over the years. No matter whether the chosen occupation is distributing leaflets, or being on hand to do odd jobs, the principle underlying the activity is the same.

Productive activity takes people out of themselves. It helps take their minds off their immediate condition and off their obsessive and unhealthy preoccupation with self. What it also does, perhaps paradoxically, is to restore a *proper* sense of self to someone whose perceptions have been damaged or distorted. In helping others they help themselves.

Paul's daughter Joanne can testify to it. 'I noticed an enormous improvement in Dad's condition soon after he joined Depression Alliance,' she says. 'It also gave him confidence to do other things. Mum's mother had died and with the help of a small inheritance we bought a house in the Forest of Dean.'

If one bears in mind that a feature of Paul's depression was agoraphobia, the significance of what follows is not to be minimised. 'We used to drive down there in convoy – taking a Transit van to carry the furniture. At one point mum and my sister had set off ahead leaving just me and Dad. That meant HE now had to drive us back. It was an enormous undertaking for him and it took us all of 10 hours. But we did it. It was one of the great turning points.'

Paul agrees. 'Buying that house was a commitment to the future. We were going to survive come what may. The sense of achievement was enormous. For once I was looking forward not back. We celebrated our silver wedding by going to Malta. Now

I have a fear of flying! But I got there somehow. I've never looked back. Being chairman of DA gave me back my self-esteem and, with the renewed confidence it gave me, I was able to put effort into buying and equipping the house.' Not for nothing is Paul fond of quoting the Chinese proverb, "The journey of a thousand miles begins with a single step".'

He also recalls a moment when his psychotherapist became uncharacteristically exasperated with him ('as any sensible person would', Paul now adds). The circumstances of the particular exchange are now forgotten but not the piece of wisdom his therapist, in his exasperation, had chosen to impart. 'Basically he told me,' says Paul, 'that ultimately my life was my own and that it was for me to muck it up or make something of it. The choice was mine. I was furious with him at the time. It hurt like hell. But he was absolutely right.'

Paul's natural skills as an administrator were extremely useful in coordinating the network of self-help groups which come under the wing of the Depression Alliance. Others who do not necessarily feel cut out to run the administrative side of things but who yet want to help in a practical way might consider other options.

One of these is to form a self-help group of one's own. Joan Gibson of the Depression Alliance was instrumental in getting Paul motivated – despite himself! It was her compassionate and understanding letters to him when he was in the grip of his darkest depressions that helped him to see there was the possibility of light somewhere. She now has advice of her own to anyone considering the formation of a self-help group:

6 A group can be a tremendous help in overcoming depression, both for the person who runs it and for those who attend. It is not a difficult undertaking. You need only be willing to ask a few others to come to your home and chat informally over a cup of tea. Group leaders are not expected to be amateur psychologists but are better described as hosts or hostesses. The great value is that all who come know that they will meet with sympathy and understanding, because everyone else has experienced depression and can offer mutual support. 9

And she adds with cautious reassurance:

❛ It is possible, while still feeling depressed, to run a group – indeed, most people find that it contributes to their recovery. But it is not advisable to attempt this if your depression/anxiety is severe. If you feel able to go ahead, the first thing to do is to find one or two others who can help, too. We all need support from time to time and we do not encourage people to go it alone. We will be able to provide some local contacts and posters for display in doctors' surgeries, local Samaritans, Citizen's Advice Bureaux etc. Don't feel you cannot run a group if it is not possible to hold meetings in your own home. Informal meetings are usually best but some groups successfully make use of a hired room or hall. ❜

And finally a word of encouragement:

❛ If at first you have a very poor response don't be discouraged. Even if no one comes to your meetings for a while, they may well be helped by knowing that the group exists. ❜

Paul Lanham speaks of the great solidarity these self-help groups can generate. There is, he says, a great reassurance knowing that the members are all in the same boat together. What is more, their experiences and their advice (freely shared by all those who wish to listen) may carry far greater conviction than some of the things a hard-pressed professional might say. Acknowledging, in the first instance, the debt he owes to Joan's letters Paul says that his involvement in the groups has taught him a number of things:

❛ I felt that someone actually cared about the fact that I was depressed and mixed up and that my world had crashed about my head. It was a wonderful surprise after groping in the dark for so long. No matter how low we may be, we belong to a unique organisation that really cares about its members' problems. You may feel that life has nothing to offer because nobody cares about you. You may feel that no one has enough patience with your problems, perhaps because you lack patience with them. Nothing could be further from the truth. The organisation is a place where members care about each other.

A second thing the group has taught me is that others really understand what is going on in my mind. We all know of the frustrations of meeting some doctors or specialists. To them our problems are abstract. But to us our state of mind hurts.

The third thing I have learnt is that I can do more than I thought I could. Within two months of contacting DA I was still at rock bottom and was invited to start a support group. No sooner was that off the ground than I was further asked to help with answering letters – a most demanding but reward-ing task. It is in these things that I have found that, although I may think I am useless, others believe I have value. One of our greatest problems lies in the lack of confidence we experi-ence when we feel depressed. This is a great pity, since such experience can be turned into a positive force. ❜

All this squares with Sally Pidd's advice. 'One of the things that's very good,' she says, 'is having a supportive network, having somebody in whom you can confide. It doesn't have to be your partner, it could be a mate down the road. It also helps to make use of people like mother and toddler groups or health visitors who are very experienced in dealing with problems associated with bringing up children.'

But involvement in self-help groups alone may not be sufficient to put an end to chronic depression. And the role of a medical practitioner may sometimes be a crucial, comple-mentary part of any 'talking therapy'. A case Dr Pidd has dealt with serves to illustrate the point.

❛I have recently been treating someone who's had a rather long postnatal depression. I saw her when the baby was 18 months old and she has really been quite severely depressed for the best part of a year. She had reached the point where she felt that not only could she not look after the baby for one more day, but that she might actually harm the baby, too. It was very difficult to enlist the family's support because, up until that time, it had not been at all sympathetic. She was made to feel that she was whining all the time. The family thought she was nothing more than a grumpy mother who should be pulling herself together. At this point I was able to intervene. ❜

What Dr Pidd was able to do was to diagnose a *medical* condition. As soon as she had done that, the picture changed and suddenly the rest of the family rallied round. The woman's mother paid for the child to attend a nursery two days a week, which gave her a break; she also invited her daughter to bring the child to her house some of the time, which ensured that the baby was safe; and the family generally pitched in to support her. The situation changed dramatically, but it was only by calling the mother 'ill' that the family could be persuaded to help. It was as if the medical diagnosis had given the family permission to sympathise. And once it was formally recognised that illness was involved the implied criticism stopped and everyone pulled together to help the mother. What was more, the family could now provide the supportive network the mother needed to persuade her that she was not alone.

In connecting with others the sufferer takes a positive step forward. If, as one sufferer has described it, depression is 'one of the loneliest illnesses known to man', then it follows that anything that can be done to relieve the loneliness will relieve the depression. Very often a person will resist such a move to join in with others on the grounds that he or she is too tired. But quite often the sensation of fatigue is an illusion. Going out and doing something with a group of people can actively reinvigorate whereas staying in bed can serve only to make the fatigue seem worse.

When depression is at its most severe, however, no such advice will be heeded. None of it gets through the impenetrable wall isolating a sufferer from the outside world. But it may be useful to have the advice lodged somewhere at the back of one's mind in readiness for the moment when the depression begins to lift.

In these windows of opportunity there are practical things to be done to establish a relationship with the world. And with that renewed relationship comes a kind of healing. Staying in isolation at home is a near certain way of increasing the sense of despondency one feels and of deepening the depression. It might be a good idea for someone coming out of depression to consider involvement in voluntary work, or in church activities.

Evening classes or part-time study may provide other ways of establishing all-important contact with the world, contact without which it is impossible to be fully human.

All this can be done in parallel with a self-help group. Indeed, it is often a good idea, in the early stages of confidence building, to have the safety net of fellow sufferers to cushion you when you stumble.

Gradually, in the company of sympathetic listeners like these, or with a loving partner, or a trusted therapist you will discover strengths that you never knew you possessed. Or rather, strengths that you always suspected were there but which, over long years of repression or of discouragement, of fear or of imagined powerlessness, of physical or emotional cruelty, you have watched slide into disuse. Those strengths can be revived. And the power to exercise control over your life can be regained once again. In the company of others a proper sense of self will grow. This is not to be confused with self-centredness nor selfishness which are essentially negative characteristics whose primary function is to cut you off from the world.

No, a proper sense of self does the opposite; it propels you into the world with the confidence to share its joys and the fortitude to bear its pains. It transforms the vulnerable and dependent child into the responsible adult whose strength comes from within. At ease with yourself you are at ease with the world. You may then find that the world becomes a surprisingly interesting place to be. And all the more interesting from the moment you discover you suddenly have a stake in it.

Finding that proper sense of self may take time but it is there to be found. It may need dusting off, it may need a bit of adjusting and fine tuning but it is there somewhere – at the bottom of an unattractive and even frightening pile of early experiences, maybe; or left behind somewhere in a past that was subsequently overshadowed by trauma. But it is there and finding it may be the most constructive and durable way of getting the upper hand over depression once and for all.

As the novelist Susan Howatch once said, 'Find the person you were always meant to be – and get on with it'.

Epilogue

We all aspire to happiness but so often it is unhappiness which makes us better people. Unhappiness induces compassion and nurtures wisdom. Depression, by contrast, does none of that.

Let us end where we began with a description of its corrosive effects:

> 6 Depression 4 me means despair, feeling there is no hope, no future and no point. I cannot C a reason 2 keep going, I want 2 run and hide, C no one, go nowhere, find a hole, curl up in it and die. Everything hurts and there is nothing I can do about it. Depression 4 me is full of paradoxes. I want 2 reach out and touch somebody but when I realise there is no one there I want 2 withdraw completely. But then when I withdraw I loathe the place I withdraw 2 and so I want 2 reach out again and that starts a vicious circle in my head. Some time in the middle of a bad bout I C nothing, everything has gone. I think of all my past, how bad everything has been, all the injustices where no one defended me. All the injustices in the world and no one there to stop them. In the midst of my silence my head screams with zillions of thoughts . . . I hate myself yet I love life and think life is wonderful – for other people, not 4 me. I look 2 my future and I can see more of the same. I feel trapped, caged, stuck – with no way out. 9
>
> *Serena*

Afam Ejimbe, who took himself to the brink of suicide but who drew back at the last moment – only seconds before slipping the noose round his neck – puts it this way:

> 6 Depression is a fatal disease. I'm constantly teetering on the edge of an abyss. I feel I've been to a dark place and seen things no one else can imagine. 9

Both testimonies hint at deep childhood hurts. In Afam's case the hurts were emotional and physical. As a child growing up in Nigeria he was a witness to his parents' endless rows, and was frequently beaten by his father for allegedly siding with his mother in any argument. 'I'm a stubborn believer in childhood shaping our fate,' he says.

Steve's experience of depression is harder to fathom but clearly stems from childhood influences. 'I've had no losses or bereavements,' he says, 'and so I think the depression goes back a long way – although I didn't have a label for it until my early 30s. I remember recently wandering past my old primary school and seeing a wire fence with a sign that said "Trespassers will be prosecuted". Then I thought "What a dump this is. You're damned if you get out and you're damned if you get in." And then I suddenly had this flashback when I got this Monday morning feeling and was taken right back to the age of eight. That's depression.'

Just as a small child was saddened by the light on Sainsbury's wall opposite Jimmy's Cafe one unremarkable Saturday morning so, too, was Steve momentarily brought low by a memory of another distant morning (this time a Monday) and a dismal walk to school. 'We are the sum total,' says Afam, 'of what we learnt from our parents and from society.'

It is a convincing explanation but not everyone will agree with it. There will be many who say that a human personality is not so simply explained; that our genetic predisposition, and our sheer biological complexity have incalculable and unforeseen effects on us all. Indeed, there is evidence of that in plenty. Why, for example, do some people survive the most appalling deprivation and others crumple at the first signs of adversity? Under such circumstances the environmental factor does little to explain things.

And yet, from our own experiences and in some mysterious, unfathomed way, we know that it explains a lot. It has something to do with attachment and loss. The attachment to the people and things of this world – which brings pleasure. And the loss of what has brought pleasure – which brings pain.

At the deepest level we want to belong to the earth and to be part of all that is in it. We long for communion. Communion with each other (and, for some, communion with God, the source of all). If we fail to achieve this or lose it once we have it, we are thrown back on ourselves and the profound loneliness that this implies is enough to induce a kind of silent despair.

The depression that can ensue at a conscious or unconscious level further cuts us off from things and makes the possibility of communion even more remote. Take this from Paul Lanham who was, you will remember, a practising Anglican priest until chronic depression forced him to retire prematurely. 'At my worst,' he says, 'I was at home sealed off in a dark room and undergoing deep sleep therapy. A Baptist lay preacher came round and said to me rather piously, "Of course you can pray your way through this despair, can't you?" and I told her she was wrong. I told her that, when you're depressed, you simply can't pray at all. And so she tiptoed away and never came back again. Religion is a two-edged sword as far as depression is concerned. In some people it can create more problems than it can solve. You think, "How can God love me when I can't love myself?" and that brings with it all manner of guilt. You then feel surrounded by people who have more faith than you. I used to feel terrible going to church.'

For all that, Paul is determined to 'make my experience of depression redemptive. I want to use what I've gone through in some sort of creative way and to put it to use for the benefit of others.'

The desire to help someone other than oneself may, in the end, represent the single most effective means of overcoming depression there is. And, crucially, it may represent the best way of preventing it in the first place. There is an African proverb which says 'it takes a village to raise a child'. The wisdom it contains is clear.

We must all, it says, take responsibility for our fellow human beings. We cannot leave their nurture to a mother or a father alone. We must be ready to fulfil the role expected of us as members of a wider family and to provide support when it is needed. If we fail to nurture a sense of belonging in the young we leave them adrift in an apparently unfriendly universe. If vulnerable children are not cared for and loved they will grow up feeling out of place in the world, ill at ease and quite possibly despairing in the face of a society which does not seem to care. The chronic depression this feeling can induce within (and, increasingly, the violence it can provoke when the anger is turned outwards) are part of the price we pay for getting things wrong.

Isolation, once again, is depression's defining characteristic. How do we climb out of the prison of depression? Terry's experience is instructive:

> ❛ I was going into town one day feeling in a reasonable sort of mood because I was having a comparatively good day. My moods had been up and down and I had just begun to emerge from a pretty bad bout of depression. I looked behind me and could see that the bus I wanted to catch was approaching so I ran to the stop. It must have been clear to the driver that I was trying to catch his bus but, even though I was only feet from the bus stop, he sailed past me and didn't stop. I felt like crying. And in that moment all the lightness of the day began to fade. I could feel myself slipping back into my depression. I was just about to turn back, go home, and curl up in bed when I saw another bus approaching. When I got on, the bus driver who might have been my guardian angel said, "I saw that, mate. Sorry about that. You should complain to the depot. Here, have this ride on the company." I felt enormously relieved and could face the day again. ❜

The moral of Terry's story is plain. Bad things happen. And these will make us depressed. Nothing will remove the experience of those bad things but other experiences can dilute their effect. Time, in other words, is the healer. Terry almost gave in to the despair induced by the selfishness of bus driver number one but he was saved by the presence, a few moments later, of bus driver number two whose friendliness won through.

But for time's healing properties to be felt we have to hang on in hope. We have to survive a day at a time, solving one problem at a time and merely endure life's pains as a prelude, we believe, to its pleasures. Sisyphus had to continue to roll his boulder up the hill even though it rolled down every time he reached the top. And for his heroic endurance and his faith in a future unknown, Camus judged him ultimately happy.

In a lighter but equally wise vein a New Yorker cartoon captured the human condition perfectly. The scene is the bedroom. It is morning. A depressed man sits on the edge of the bed unable to motivate himself even to stand up. His eyes are heavy, his face is drawn. He is on the edge of despair. His wife stands in front of him determined not to see him crumble and says, cruel but kind, 'What do you mean you've nothing to live for? What about the mortgage and the school fees?' Life is hard but it has its rewards.

Psychiatrists like Sally Pidd will make their medical diagnoses and continue to prescribe the medicines which will alleviate the symptoms of depression. Their contribution is incalculable. But even she knows from long experience that sometimes there is little more to do, after all else has been tried, than to put an arm round their shoulder and weep in sympathy.

The healing power of this simple human gesture is not to be ignored. A theologian tells the story of a mother waking in the night to hear her small child in distress in the bedroom next door. She goes in and puts her arm round the frightened child and says those comforting words, 'There, there. It's all right. Mummy's here.' But is she lying when she says this? Of course, Mummy is there. But are things *really* all right in a world that has war, violence, envy, cancer, greed? The theologian concludes that this is no lie after all. The presence of another human being in the world *makes* it all right. All, in the end, shall be well.

For believers and non-believers alike the encouragement in the Book of Joshua contains a consoling truth: 'Be strong and of a good courage; be not afraid, neither be thou dismayed: for the Lord thy God is with thee, whithersoever thou goest.' In other words, and more prosaically, 'You do not have to be alone.'

Acknowledgements

I am indebted to many individuals and organisations for the help and advice they gave in so short a time. Of these I should like principally to thank:

Depression Alliance; The Royal College of Psychiatrists; The Priory Hospital; The Manic Depression Fellowship; Depressives Anonymous.

For the Samaritans: Simon Armson, Elisabeth Salisbury, Jenny Cunnington, Joan Guénault, and Paul Farmer.

Dr André Tylee for his straightforward and patient summary of a lifetime's work.

And, chiefly, Dr Sally Pidd, Honorary Consultant Psychiatrist to The Samaritans, without whose clear, concise and sensible advice this book could not have been written. I have done my best to summarise the medical detail accurately and any short-comings are mine alone.

Finally those (mostly) anonymous men and women who have had the courage to open their hearts to a complete stranger, and to share their stories with honesty and insight.

And . . .
Thank you, Lorna. Thank you, Jo. Thank you, Isabelle. Thank you, Paul. Thank you, David. Thank you, Sue.

Further Reading

Acting As Friends: The Story of The Samaritans, Michael de la Noy (Constable, 1987)

Answers to Suicide, The Samaritans (Constable, 1978)

Before I Die Again, Chad Varah (Constable, 1992)

Behind The Mask: Men, Feelings and Suicide, The Samaritans (The Samaritans, 1995)

Breaking the Bonds, Dorothy Rowe (HarperCollins)

Caring For The Suicidal, John Eldrid (Constable, 1987)

Climbing Out of Depression, Sue Atkinson (Lion)

The Costs of Suicide: Ripples On The Pond, The Samaritans (The Samaritans, 1994)

Depression: The Way Out Of Your Prison, Dorothy Rowe (Routledge and Kegan Paul)

I Can't Face Tomorrow: Help For Those With Thoughts of Suicide and Those Who Counsel Them, Norman Kier (Thorsons, 1986)

The Samaritans: Befriending The Suicidal, Chad Varah, ed. (Constable, 1985)

Useful Addresses

ACT (Action for the care of families whose Children have life-threatening and Terminal conditions)
The Institute of Child Health
Royal Hospital for Sick Children
Bristol BS2 8BJ
Tel: 01272 221556

Age Concern
Astral House
1268 London Rd
London
Tel: 0181 679 8000

Al-Anon Family Groups
61 Great Dover Street
London SE1 4YF
Tel: 0171 403 0888

Alcoholics Anonymous
General Service Office
P O Box 1
Stonebow House
Stonebow
York YO1 2NJ
Tel: 01904 644026

BAC
British Association for Counselling
1 Regents Place
Rugby
Warwickshire CV21 3BX
Tel: 01788 78328/9

BACUP (Cancer)
121–3 Charterhouse St
London EC1M 6AA
Tel: 0171 608 1661
Outside London: 0800 181199

Cancer Link
17 Britannia Street
London WC1X 9JN
Tel: 0171 833 2451

Compassionate Friends
53 North Street
Bristol BS3 1EN
Helpline: 01179 539639
Admin: 01179 665202

CRUSE Bereavement Care
Cruse House
126 Sheen Rd
Richmond
Surrey TW9 1UR
Tel: 0181 332 7227

Depression Alliance
P O Box 1022
London SE1 7QB
Tel: 0171 721 7672

Depressives Anonymous
36 Chestnut Avenue
Beverley
North Humberside HU17 7QU
Tel: 0482 860619

Gingerbread
16/17 Clerkenwell Close
London EC1R 0AA
Tel: 0171 336 8183

Hospice Information
St Christopher's Hospice
51–59 Lawrie Park Road
London SE26 6DZ
Tel: 0181 778 9525

Manic Depression Fellowship
8–10 High Street
Kingston-Upon-Thames
Surrey KT1 1EY
Tel: 0181 974 6550

MIND (National Association for
Mental Health)
Granta House
15–19 Broadway
Stratford
London E15 4BQ
Tel: 0181 519 2122

National AIDS Helpline
Tel: 0800 657123

National Childbirth Trust
Alexandra House
Oldham Terrace
London W3 6NH
Tel: 0181 992 8637

Relate (formerly The National
Marriage Guidance Bureau)
Herbert Gray College
Little Church Street
Rugby CV21 3AP
Tel: 01788 573241

The Samaritans
10 The Grove
Slough
Berks SL1 1QP
Helpline: 0345 909090
Admin: 01753 532713

SANDS (Stillbirth and Neo-Natal
Death Society)
28 Portland Place
London W1N 3DE
Tel: 0171 436 5881

Seasonal Affective Disorder
Association
P O Box 989
London SW7 2PZ

Terrence Higgins Trust
52–54 Grays Inn Rd
London WC1X 8JU
Helpline: 0171 242 1010
Admin: 0171 831 0330

Index

Also from Vermilion

ANXIETY AND DEPRESSION
A practical guide to recovery
Professor Robert Priest

Feelings of anxiety and depression confront us all from time to time, and can vary in their severity. Recognising the symptoms, understanding their causes and effects, and knowing what help is available can be very reassuring, and help to overcome the condition.

Professor Priest has written this book to provide help for those feeling anxious and depressed. He covers practical self help methods of reducing stress and offers an explanation of the causes and effects of anxiety and depression. This book provides up-to-date information on the professional help available and details the action and side-effects of medication.

- - - - ✂ -

To order the above title direct from Vermilion (p&p free), use this form or call our credit-card hotline on **01279 427203**.

Please send me _____ copies of **ANXIETY AND DEPRESSION**
@ £8.99 each   ISBN 0 09 181266 6

Mr/Ms/Mrs/Miss/Other _____

Address: _____

_____

Postcode: _____   Signed: _____

HOW TO PAY

I enclose a cheque/postal order for £ _____ made payable to 'VERMILION'

I wish to pay by Access/Visa card (delete where appropriate)

Card No: _____   Expiry Date: _____

Post order to **Murlyn Services Ltd, PO Box 50, Harlow, Essex CM17 0DZ**.

POSTAGE AND PACKING ARE FREE. Offer open in Great Britain including Northern Ireland. Books should arrive less than 28 days after we receive your order; they are subject to availability at time of ordering. If not entirely satisfied return in the same packaging and condition as received with a covering letter within 7 days. Vermilion books are available from all good booksellers.